THE DIVERSE SOCIETY:
Implications for Social Policy

The Diverse SOCIETY:

IMPLICATIONS For Social Policy

*Pastora San Juan Cafferty
and Leon Chestang, Editors*

NATIONAL ASSOCIATION OF SOCIAL WORKERS
1425 H STREET, N.W.
WASHINGTON, D.C. 20005

Cover and text design by Jeanette Portelli

Copyright © 1976 by the National Association of Social Workers, Inc.

International Standard Book No.: 0–87101–072–0

Library of Congress Catalog Card No.: 76–43633

NASW Publication No.: CBC–072–C

Printed in U.S.A.

3

Contents

Preface

This book is the product of a study group created at the School of
Social Service Administration at the University of Chicago and funded
by the Ford Foundation. The group's purpose was to study ethnicity
and race in American society. Joining us on the study group's panel
were Leonard Borman, Leona Grossman, and Dolores Norton—all three
authors of essays in this volume—as well as Arthur Mann, Preston
and Sterling Morton Professor in the Department of History at the
University of Chicago, and Donnell Pappenfort, Professor in the
School of Social Service Administration at the University of Chicago.
As members of this group, all participated in the discussions that
generated these writings, helped define the contents of the book, and,
together, acted as an editorial board. Each author, in turn, enthu-
siastically worked with us in carrying out the research and writing
and then patiently edited so that the final volume would constitute
a coherent statement rather than merely a series of papers.

It is impossible to acknowledge and express appreciation to all
who have influenced our thinking and who have in this way contributed to the writing of this book. Special gratitude, however, goes
to Reverend Andrew Greeley, whose valuable work and generous
counsel have shaped our own understanding of ethnic phenomena,
and to Joan Durman, who, as research assistant to the study group,
was responsible for the administration of the group's work and whose
valuable insights contributed significantly to the ideas expressed in
this volume.

Pastora San Juan Cafferty
Leon Chestang

Chicago, 1976

Introduction

Any serious attempt to come to terms with ethnicity as a social phenomenon and with its relation to the institutional structures of American society involves an enormous challenge to research, theory, and social planning. The concept of ethnicity may be viewed on multiple levels. In its deepest sense, ethnicity is imbedded in the development of selfhood. The perceptual experiences, shared symbolisms, oral traditions, feelings, and sentiments that make up ethnicity are learned early in the processes of socialization. Greeley, elaborating on concepts from Clifford Geertz and Harold Isaacs, speaks of it in terms of "primordial attachments," a sense of belonging and self-validation, a part of man's prerational past.[1]

At the sociocognitive level, ethnic identification takes on a group dimension. Those with common national, racial, or religious origins share a sense of "peoplehood" and define themselves as such: "I am a Polish Catholic, or an Irish Protestant, a Russian Jew," and the like. At such times, one is identified as a member of a particular in-group, which is structurally and culturally different from the out-group.

Not all persons who share common ethnic memories or common symbols, or who even speak the same language, identify themselves with a specific ethnic group. They may ignore or reject their ethnic origins if given this choice by society. However, much of their individual behavior continues to be related to ethnic origins even when these origins are not acknowledged.

Ethnic group identity is thus more than a condition of common biological and historical origins, and of shared language, traditions, sentiments, and cultural networks. It is also a form of self-conceptual-

[1] Andrew Greeley, "The Rediscovery of Ethnics," *Antioch Review*, 31 (Fall 1971), p. 347.

ization that the individual takes on himself or that others assign to him or force upon him.[2] This is an important point. There is no guarantee that a shared ethnic heritage produces homogeneity of thought, feeling, behavior, or group loyalty. The same ethnic identity may have different meanings to its different bearers. Certain features of ethnic identity are deeply imbedded and persist even after experience has shown them to be dysfunctional; other aspects of ethnicity may be easily shed or are subject to change over time. The strength of a person's identification with his ethnic origins is also influenced by situational factors; in periods of stress or threat some people return to the familiar sources of comfort and help that are available in an ethnic enclave. These voluntary and involuntary aspects of ethnicity are what make this subject so complex.

Some ethnic enclaves preserve their cultural systems by isolating themselves or rejecting the dominant society. The Amish, the Hasidic Jews, and the Mennonites, for example, can be rightfully described as "ethnic sects." These groups, through powerful internal social controls, have erected sociological walls even though they may, like the Hasidic Jews, dwell in busy inner cities and are surrounded by differing ethnic groups with whom they are compelled to interact constantly. In rural environments, the attempts of such ethnic groups to preserve their boundaries are not accompanied by the same conscious efforts at separating themselves from other groups.

Many ethnic groups in the United States have experienced prejudice, discrimination, and exploitation. The treatment of an ethnic group by the majority society is often dependent on the group's social and economic position. The Irish immigrants to Boston, at first completely excluded and discriminated against, achieved political control and acceptance within three generations. In the case of the Jews in New York City, a certain cultural and social domination makes them the in-group despite their status as a numerical minority. Yet the Mexican-Americans in the Southwest, although they inhabited the territory long before it was annexed by the United States, have been segregated socially and economically for over a century.

Some groups remain trapped as ethnic minorities in a "subculture of poverty," behaviorally defined by Lewis.[3] The influence of class and ethnicity on behavioral patterning is a complex issue, which has

[2] Michael Novak, *The Rise of the Unmeltable Ethnics* (New York: Macmillan Co., 1973).

[3] Oscar Lewis, "The Culture of Poverty," *Scientific American* (October 1966), pp. 19–25.

been vehemently debated by sociologists and anthropologists. Identical behavior may be interpreted as attributable to cultural life styles or to reactions to poverty and feelings of alienation. Burma has termed these two contrasting approaches the "subcultural" and the "nonsubcultural" schools of thought.[4] The subcultural school holds that grim, stressful, and depriving environments elicit similar responses from people despite cultural differences and that the "subculture of poverty" thus cuts across all ethnic groups. The other school argues that reactions to stress differ from one ethnic group to another and that these reactions run counter to the categorizations of Lewis's subcultural school. Burma argues that evidence for the nonsubcultural point of view may be seen among Mexican-Americans.

Gordon presents a penetrating discussion of the relationship between ethnicity and social class.[5] He believes that each ethnic group may contain within it some or all the social classes found in the society. He has created the term *ethclass* to denote the subsociety created by the intersection of ethnicity and social class—lower-middle-class Irish Catholic, for example. Gordon further defines two types of identification: historical, which has as its locus the ethnic group, and participational, which is the ethclass. Members of similar ethnic groups but different social classes share "peoplehood" (historical identification) but do not necessarily have similar behavioral styles (participational identification).

America is a nation of ethnic groups. The idea of cultural pluralism was embedded in the ideology of the Founding Fathers. Historically, however, the pressure has been toward conformity to an Anglo-Saxon ideal. Greeley cites the colloquial expression of this melting-pot model as "Why can't they be like us?"[6] Theories of assimilation for years gave support to this pressure for conformity and helped shape many national policies and institutions. But in spite of the melting-pot theory, ethnic pluralism has prevailed as a reality. It is the very fabric of American society.

Cultural diversity has indeed flourished at different periods in

[4] John H. Burma, "A Comparison of the Mexican American Subculture with the Oscar Lewis Culture of Poverty Model," in Thomas E. Lasswell, John H. Burma, and Sidney H. Bronson, eds., *Life in Society* (Glenview, Ill.: Scott, Foresman and Co., 1970), pp. 694–698.

[5] Milton M. Gordon, *Assimilation in American Life* (New York: Oxford University Press, 1964), pp. 47, 51, and 53.

[6] Andrew Greeley, *Why Can't They Be Like Us?* (New York: E. P. Dutton & Co., 1971).

American history. Current ethnic affirmations, assertive group actions, and cultural revivals attest to the fact that ethnics are "unmeltable." [7] At other times, the assimilationist ideology has been a way of asserting majority group power even though the objective of its originators might originally have been to assure equality. This, in essence, is the paradox of pluralism in America: the American people, a nation of immigrants, remain ambivalent about the value of ethnic pluralism.

This paradox is best examined in the writings of Milton Gordon, who reworks and sharpens the assimilation concept in his discussion of structural and cultural pluralism.[8] Structural pluralism strengthens the ethnic group by supporting the values, relationship patterns, behaviors, and even material artifacts of a culture. Although the goal of cultural pluralism is to guarantee some continuity for each ethnic group, it does so without creating interference in American civic activities. It allows for exchange, negotiation, and reciprocity without the liquidation of identity. In Gordon's analysis, the key to any understanding of the ethnic make-up of American society is structural pluralism. Structural assimilation, on the other hand, is a sign that "the will to live" has died.

Only if the reality of ethnic diversity in American society is recognized and incorporated into the creation and implementation of social policy can such policies be effective. The fact is, however, that theories of assimilation have long dominated the formulation of public policies. Public school systems were created to teach American democracy and English to the children of immigrants. Although educational policy is perhaps the most clearly articulated statement of assimilationist policy, it is not the only one. National and local policies are made with little recognition of differences among ethnic groups. Despite such disregard for its cultural heritage, each immigrant people struggled to retain its traditions. There is constant and continuing evidence that ethnicity is important in defining individual and community identity; there is further rich evidence that the behavior of individuals, and of communities, is greatly influenced by ethnic identity.

Public policies must respond to the reality of society. To ignore this reality results, at best, in making such policies ineffective; worse, it might destroy the fabric of community. The writings in this book do not suggest that public policy in America respond only to ethnic diversity, ignoring the common values that make up a specifically

[7] Novak, op. cit., p. vii.
[8] Gordon, op. cit., pp. 132–159.

American consciousness. The ideal lies somewhere between assimilation and ethnic diversity. The degree to which one assimilates differs greatly among ethnic groups and among the individuals in these groups. Specific public policies at the national, state, and local levels need to be flexible in their response to ethnic diversity among the individuals and groups affected; they cannot be so constructed that they are as inflexible in their insistence on diversity as they have heretofore been in their insistence on assimilation

This flexibility must exist at both the local and the national levels. Successful local politicians have long recognized the importance of responding to special needs of ethnic communities. Long before American political parties began struggling with such notions as affirmative action and quotas, local politicians offered so-called balanced tickets to the electorate. The fabled political machines were built by precinct captains who were sensitive to ethnic loyalties. On the national level, ethnicity has been given similar attention in the appointment of cabinet members and Supreme Court justices.

Public policy and programs should also reflect these sensitivities. Since society is only served as its individual members are served, it is an accepted fact that public service agencies should interpret their programs to suit the individual. It can thus be argued that a key to what the individual is looking for is an acknowledgment of his ethnic identity.

Just as it is dangerous to ignore an individual's ethnic identity, it is equally dangerous to assume certain behavioral characteristics based on that identity. Public agencies must respond to ethnic differences without substituting the rigidity of ethnic stereotypes for the rigidity of assumed majority values. That is to say, a sensitive emergency room staff would not ignore a complaining Italian on the assumption that all Italians complain and give priority to a complaining Irishman on the assumption that for an Irishman to complain something must really be wrong. Rather, they would respond to the needs of both individuals, aware that each is different as an individual, that ethnic identity is a significant factor in individual identity but that it does not necessarily define it.

In the formulation of national policies, sensitivity to ethnic identity is imperative but difficult to achieve. To make a public health program responsive to the values of the ethnic community requires sensitivity. To make public health legislation responsive to national ethnic diversity requires a recognition of this diversity and an understanding of its implications for policy formulation.

The studies of ethnic identity are few, and there is little understanding of its meaning. Recent research demonstrates the persistence of ethnic cohesion over long periods of time. However, for all the talk of a resurgence of ethnic identity, the fact is that ethnic studies lack the respectability to command the attention of many serious scholars. When Glazer and Moynihan wrote *Beyond the Melting Pot* in 1963, they described it as "a beginning book"; in the preface to the 1970 edition, they decried the dearth of ethnic studies during the decade of the sixties.[9] Unfortunately, those who make public policies cannot wait for the findings of scholarly research, nor can they ignore ethnic reality simply because it is not fully understood.

This also is "a beginning book." It is meant as another step in the direction of recognizing the importance of ethnicity in the formulation of public policies.

Each essay in this book is intended to do two things: to show the diversity of culture in American society and to examine how a social policy can be made to respond to this diversity. The policy recommendations range from those addressing education to those concerning housing and labor, but no attempt is made to deal with all public policy issues. Each essay is simply an argument for the necessity of acknowledging American ethnic diversity in the formulation and implementation of public policies. The essays are intended to provoke questions rather than to answer them, to encourage research and study both by the makers of public policy and by those who implement policy.

[9] Nathan Glazer and Daniel P. Moynihan, *Beyond the Melting Pot: The Negroes, Puerto Ricans, Jews, Italians, and Irish of New York City* (Cambridge, Mass.: M.I.T. Press, 1970), pp. xxvi-xxxii.

part one

ETHNICITY IN AMERICA

Why Study Ethnicity?

ANDREW M. GREELEY

Andrew M. Greeley, Ph.D., is Director, Center for the Study of American Pluralism, National Opinion Research Center, University of Chicago, Chicago, Illinois.

A friend of a colleague was born in Hungary but had moved to a Western European country. Finally, after twenty years, he had saved enough money to purchase for himself a second-class citizenship. He summoned all his friends together for a massive celebration of the fact that he was now, at last, permitted to devote his life's savings toward purchasing his citizenship.

Another incident concerns a man born in Czechoslovakia of German and Czech parents. He married a German from the Sudetenland, applied for citizenship in West Germany, and was turned down because he and his wife spoke to one another frequently in Czech.

Most Americans are shocked to the point of disbelief when they hear such stories. They take it for granted that access to citizenship for immigrants is a matter of course in other societies, just as it is in their own. In fact, they are reluctant to have people within their borders who do not apply for citizenship, while other countries are reluctant to grant it. Other nations jealously guard citizenship; Americans vigorously insist that all should assume it.

In the United States little attention is paid to the plight of the "guest workers" in the Western European social democracies. Whether

they be from Africa, Yugoslavia, or Italy, the guest workers are permitted to stay only for a brief period of time, are generally not
allowed to bring their families, and are excluded from citizenship.
Such practices seem so incredible to Americans that they simply ignore
them. One hears frequently, for example, how "progressive" and
"enlightened" the Swedes are, how much Americans should learn from
them. Yet for all their progress and enlightenment, the Swedes would
not treat Italian guest workers as anything more than outcasts, who
are not welcome and are never permitted to become citizens.

Few Americans have thought it particularly worthwhile to understand why United States citizenship is so accessible to immigrants
when in most North Atlantic countries it is rarely conceded to foreign-
ers, and then only under the most rigorous conditions. As Mann has
suggested, the Founding Fathers, political philosophers that they were,
were conscious of the need for an intellectual and cultural base for
their new nation.[1] Such a base could not be religious because the
society was already denominationally pluralistic: Congregationalist in
New England, Quaker in Pennsylvania, Anglican in New York and
Virginia, Methodist and Baptist in the South. Nor could the cultural
basis for the society be ethnic; for even at the time of the Revolutionary
War at least half the population was not Anglo-Saxon, but Scotch-
Irish, German, and black. Nor could the common basis be a unique
cultural heritage; for although Hastings, the Magna Carta, the War
of the Roses, and the Glorious Revolution meant something to the
Anglo-Saxons, it meant much less, if anything, to the rest of the
population.

LOFTY PRINCIPLES

Consequently, the Founding Fathers decided—as the early naturalization laws make clear—that the central core of beliefs which would
create the American nation would consist of certain political principles
contained in the Declaration of Independence and the Constitution.
Citizenship would be granted to the man willing to be a citizen in
the Enlightenment sense of the word, that is to say, a man who
committed himself to the eighteenth-century political principles en-
shrined in the Declaration of Independence and the Constitution. No
one could be excluded from citizenship whatever his religion, his
ethnicity, or his heritage so long as he was willing to pledge allegiance
to these political principles.

[1] Conversations with Arthur Mann, University of Chicago, 1974.

Jefferson and Madison might have been shocked at the thought that within less than a century forty-five million new immigrants would come to the shores of the United States, while at the same time the population expanded across the continent. Yet, the Americans, however grudgingly, did indeed admit the immigrants, requiring, in theory at least, only that they pledge allegiance to the established political system to achieve equal rights as citizens. This theory may have been flawed, but it was flawed in practice, not in statement. The gathering in of the nations to construct the American republic within a single century is among the most extraordinary phenomena of modern history. What is incredible is not that there has been injustice and violence in the history of the country, but that the country has held together at all.

FLAWS IN THE AMERICAN EXPERIMENT

The problems were certain and obvious. Neither the blacks nor the American Indians were given an opportunity to become citizens. Orientals were admitted for a time, but then excluded. Eastern and southern Europeans were admitted by the millions until the American republic quavered and departed from its principles of equal access to citizenship and established discriminatory quota systems to keep these "inferior" peoples from contaminating the American stock. German-Americans were forced to pay a heavy cultural price for their origins during the two world wars. Japanese-Americans were herded into concentration camps during World War II. Finally, although in theory immigrants were not required to give up either their language or their culture, in practice the social pressures were so strong that languages were lost and cultures were repressed. More than commitment to political democracy was necessary in order to be fully accepted as an American. Despite lofty principles, the facts of the matter were that names had to be changed, accents hidden, and cultural pasts forgotten. Sometimes even religion had to be denied before the American elite would acknowledge the children and the grandchildren of immigrants as really American.

But the national creed kept Americans uneasy about these transgressions. The Immigration Act of 1965 eliminated quotas against Orientals and eastern and southern Europeans. While injustice against blacks and American Indians remains, fewer people support it, and major efforts are being made to eliminate it. More recently, as a result of the black emphasis on cultural diversity, the country has at last begun to come to terms with the religious, racial, ethnic, and geographic diversity that exists within its boundaries.

The Spanish-speaking immigrants may succeed where the Germans and the Poles failed. They may be able to remain bilingual. The theory is that one need only subscribe to American political democracy; it does not demand that one speak only English—though it does state, at least implicitly, that one should be able to speak English in addition to whatever other language one chooses. It is questionable whether that bilingualism can survive in the United States, but at present, considerable numbers of Americans are willing to admit that there is nothing "un-American" about it.

Despite its flaws, the American experiment in pluralism has in many ways been successful. Compared to the ethnic, religious, and racial conflicts in Indonesia, Ceylon, India, Bangladesh, Iraq, Burma, Cypress, Israel, Yugoslavia, and Northern Ireland, there has been astonishingly little conflict and violence in American society. Despite its large population, its immense geography, and the variegated origins of its citizenry, the United States has had only one civil war, and that was basically a conflict between two Anglo-Saxon groups. Scotch-Irish and Celtic-Irish in the United States get along reasonably well, while in Ulster they still shoot at one another. The United Kingdom may be a far more civilized place than the United States, as many of those who criticize this country from within are only too happy to point out, but that Celt and Saxon are at peace with each other here surely must be considered a better condition than the conflict in Ulster.

NEITHER MELTING POT NOR MOSAIC

But why, despite its flaws and failures, its hesitations and compromises in the face of all the centrifugal forces that could have torn it apart so easily, has the American republic held together? Perhaps no one knows. Americans have been so absorbed by self-criticism and negative comparisons with Sweden and other nations that they have not bothered to study the reasons behind their curious solidity in the face of so much diversity.

America is not, after all, a "melting pot" in Zangwill's sense of the term.[2] Some ethnics may have "melted," despite Novak's theory, but

---

[2] Israel Zangwill, *The Melting-Pot, Drama in Four Acts* (New York: The Macmillan Co., 1910).

many have not, and the "melting" does not seem to have noticeably decreased the diversity in the society.[3] On the other hand, neither does the society have Horace Kallen's "cultural pluralism" because there is intermarriage and a common language.[4] Nor is America a "pillarized" society like Ireland, Holland, Belgium, or Canada. There is no such thing as a Polish community or a black community or an Italian community in the United States as there is a Catholic community in the north of Ireland, a Flemish community in Belgium, or a French community in Canada. Geography, social class, religion, politics, or profession are not coterminous with nationality. There are Jews who are not particularly rich, Irishmen who are not particularly active politically, Polish Republicans, Italian Protestants, black conservatives —and all in reasonably substantial numbers. If the ethnic background of a person is known, it is possible to predict with some degree of confidence a number of his other characteristics, but these can be wrong frequently enough to make it obvious that American society is not a mosaic of various ethnic groups with impermeable boundaries separating them.

Except for a few people, religion, race, and ethnicity are only a component of identity and do not exhaust it. The pertinent question is not whether America has cultural pluralism in Kallen's sense, but rather this: Under what circumstances do what kinds of people fall back on their ethnic consciousness? And under what circumstances does an ethnic heritage affect attitudes, values, and behavior? Is ethnicity important in the choice of a mate, a poker partner, a psychiatrist, undertaker, insurance representative, construction contractor, priest, or political candidate? Are there times when ethnicity unconsciously influences behavior? Why are the Irish the most politicized of American ethnic groups? Why are the Poles the most likely to vote? Why do Jews in disproportionate numbers choose medicine as a career, and Germans science and engineering? Why do the Irish drink so much and the Jews and Italians so little? Why do the Irish have high morale and the Italians low morale? Why do the Irish have a high sense of political efficacy and the Jews little of such feelings? The questions are endless and leave no doubt that ethnicity is still important in American society. Yet correlations between ethnicity, on the one hand, and attitudes and behavior on the other are

[3] Michael Novak, *The Rise of the Unmeltable Ethnics: Politics and Culture in the Seventies* (New York: The Macmillan Co., 1973).

[4] Horace Kallen, *Cultural Pluralism and the American Idea: An Essay in Social Philosophy* (Philadelphia: University of Pennsylvania Press, 1956).

all relatively modest—of about the same order of magnitude as social class. Ethnicity, in other words, is important, but not all important.

If neither the melting pot nor the cultural pluralism model is a particularly useful way of looking at American society, then what models are available? It is a society of ethnic groups, each group a collectivity based on presumed common origin, which shapes to some extent the attitudes and behaviors of those who share that origin, and with which certain people may freely choose to identify at certain times of their lives.

WAY OF BEING AMERICAN

The words are all carefully chosen. First, ethnicity is a way of being American. Immigrants did not arrive as ethnics; they became such on the shores of their new country. It scarcely made sense to have "Irish" or "Italian" be an important component of one's identity when everyone else was Irish or Italian. In the country of origin people defined themselves in terms of region, province, and town. Only in this country did the immigrant come upon those who were not Irish or not Italian, or not Polish, or not Norwegian; and here such a form of self-definition takes on importance as a way of distinguishing one's own group from others in the society. It also provided a modality by which the immigrant could become part of the society. Only to a minor extent did the ethnic group represent a way of looking back at a previous heritage. It was, in a more important sense, a way of looking forward, of finding one's place in the American heritage. Even concern with national freedom in one's country of origin was justified in terms of its impact on American society. The American Irish, for example, supported the Irish nationalist movements because, it was argued, they would only fully be accepted in the United States when Ireland could be numbered among the free nations. Irish nationalism thus became a way of being American.

Similarly, the intense patriotism among the American ethnic—once so quickly ridiculed by the young and the radical—can be understood only in light of the fact that for most immigrants the right to own property and the right to vote were realized for the first time in this country. An ethnic might be legitimately proud of his heritage, but he had no illusion that the ancestral lands provided more freedom or more opportunity than the United States. Quite the contrary, this gratitude to the United States was a direct result of the assumption that the United States had made it possible for the immigrants to be both free and prosperous. The eastern and southern European Catholics are the most likely to vote of any American ethnic group. In all likelihood it is because they were the ones least likely to be enfranchised in the old country.[5] Voting is an important way of symbolizing their Americanness; and their ethnicity, from their point of view, is as American as anything else—and frequently more so.

Second, the definition of an ethnic group given here insists on the presence of cultural heritage that influences attitudes, values, personality, and behavior, even if the people influenced are unconscious of the impact of the past on the present. The Irish have been in the United States longer than most ethnic groups and are probably the least concerned with their ancestral past. They have become, in most visible ways, quite indistinguishable from middle-class Anglo-Saxons, yet on widely varying measures of activity, behavior, attitude, value, and personality, the Irish are profoundly and radically different from other groups in American society.[6] If a uniquely Irish heritage can survive three and sometimes four generations in the United States, there is no reason to think other heritages will melt away quickly.

Third, in terms of conscious self-definition, ethnicity is an option. It is available for those who choose it; but in the United States, in principle at least, no one can be compelled to be an ethnic either by members of his own group or by members of any other group. Of course, the principle is frequently violated. Blacks are judged to be black whether they want to be or not. To some extent, it is still impossible to cease being Jewish. But clearly, the ideal toward which the American creed strains is that every man ought to be free to identify with his heritage or to reject all conscious ethnic identification. The racial problem will be solved in the United States when "blackness"—as a form of self-definition—is an option that a person is free to exercise or not.

Finally, it must be observed that this definition admits the possibility of considerable pluralism within an ethnic group. Eastern Europeans in the United States, for example, are usually split into two groups, those who arrived before World War II and those who came after. The Czechs are divided into three groups: pre-World War II, 1948 refugees, and 1968 refugees. When studying diversities within groups, it is tempting to comment that in some cases there is

[5] *See* Andrew M. Greeley, *Ethnicity in the United States: A Preliminary Reconnaissance* (New York: John Wiley & Sons, 1975).

[6] Ibid.

as much pluralism within the groups as there is between them and the rest of society. The ethnic collectivity, then, derives from the simple fact that because of the diverse origins of the American people, a particular national, religious, or racial background becomes a predicate variable that an individual may on occasion choose to make an explicit part of his self-definition. How this has come to be and how it functions in practice are research questions to which American social science should devote considerable time, resources, and energy in the decades ahead.

STRATEGY OF MILITANT ETHNICITY

Within this context, what is to be said about the current emphasis on "militant ethnicity"? First, the data collected at the National Opinion Research Center indicate that the militant ethnic approach has limited appeal.[7] With the exception of the nonwhite groups, no group in American society experiences the degree of oppression that would make substantial numbers of its members sympathetic to a militant political and social style. This does not mean that militant leaders do not have an important role to play. It merely means that they do not and cannot speak for substantial segments of the constituencies they may claim.

Second, to the extent that the strategy of militant ethnicity presumes a pillarized society, this strategy is simply inaccurate in its reading of the social structure of the United States. The society would be pillarized only if, for example, the overwhelming majority of Italians constantly thought of themselves as Italian and if being Italian became the form of identity they chose for themselves almost exclusively of all other forms. It may be questioned whether such an extreme form of self-definition would be a positive influence, but such a question is purely academic. No serious scrutiny of contemporary American society indicates that this kind of one-sided self-definition is likely to be adopted.

Militant leaders may raise the level of ethnic consciousness to some degree, and this may produce positive results. They may promote greater pride in the heritage, and this is certainly good. They may occasionally mobilize political pressure, and whether that is good or not depends on the direction of the pressure. They may succeed in forming coalitions that improve the quality of urban life; and

[7] Ibid.

no one could deny the importance of that achievement. But militant ethnic leaders cannot transform the United States into a mosaic society, and to the extent that they think they can, they merely deceive themselves.

Finally, if militant ethnicity scapegoats Anglo-Saxon Protestants for the sum total of American societal ills, then it is un-American, for Anglo-Saxons are no more culpable than blacks, or Jews, or Slavs, or Italians, or any other group. Further, to assign all Anglo-Saxon Protestants, whether they be from Massachusetts, Tennessee, Texas, or California, to a single category is intolerable oversimplification.

How should the ethnic revival be evaluated? Perhaps it should first be stated that there is no ethnic revival. The ethnic groups are where they always have been—on the northwest side of Chicago, in Hamtramck, in South Boston, in Queens, the Bronx, Staten Island. There is no particular evidence that they are any more militant, or outraged, or that they feel any more oppressed than they did in the past. Instead of an ethnic revival, there is rather an arrival of consciousness of ethnicity. People have become conscious not of the ethnics themselves, but of their more vocal leaders and of the journalists and scholars who monitor American culture. If there is an ethnic revival at all, it is among Americans as a whole, who have rediscovered the diversity in their society. Although this rediscovery is admirable, one might pause to wonder why it took so long.

DIVERSITY AS A NATIONAL RESOURCE

What direction will the ethnic revival take? Two things seem to be happening. First, it is necessary to understand the various ethnic traditions of American society and also the processes, protocols, rituals, and implicit accommodations by which these groups have coexisted without major violence and conflict for a sustained period of time. That only one major sociological study has been done on the American Poles—Thomas and Znaniecki's *Polish Peasant in Europe and America*—is astonishing.[8] That that book was written more than fifty years ago is even more astonishing. Ignorance of the various ethnic traditions in the United States is an incredible piece of irresponsibility on the part of social science.

But in addition to understanding themselves and each other,

---

[8] W. I. Thomas and Florian Znaniecki, *Polish Peasant in Europe and America* (Boston: The Gorham Press, 1920).

Americans should also enjoy the diversity of their cultural heritages. That enjoyment should include more than just periodic visits to ethnic restaurants, as pleasurable as such gustatory explorations may be. Americans are all richer because the Jews have shared their literary, cultural, and comic tradition with the rest of the country, but there are additional riches of cultural heritage locked up in the eastern and southern European neighborhoods that still exist in American cities. These ethnic heritages are priceless resources. That most Americans have been uninterested in them and have, perhaps without realizing it, pressured those who possess such heritages to forget them is an unconscionable waste.

The day may come when those who are most affluent and hence have the most freedom of choice about where to live will deliberately and consciously choose to live in communities where there is a maximum of racial, religious, national, and cultural diversity. They will argue that by providing their children with an opportunity to grow up amid such diversity, they are giving them an educational experience more important than college. It will mean that Americans will have to acknowledge not merely that they have something to learn from the Jews and the blacks—and many elite Americans are ready to admit that now—but that they also have something to learn from the Poles, the Italians, the Slovaks, Lithuanians, Hungarians, Armenians, Crimean Tartars, Russian Germans, and even (heaven save us all!) from the Irish.

Social Utilities in a Pluralistic Society

WILLIAM McCREADY

William McCready, Ph.D., is Associate Program Director, Center for the Study of American Pluralism, National Opinion Research Center, University of Chicago, Chicago, Illinois.

EDITORS' COMMENT

Greeley has described the special characteristics of pluralism in American society. The implications of this pluralism for those devising and implementing social service delivery is ex-examined by McCready in the context of the political history of American ethnic communities.

Each group in a pluralistic society develops its own agenda for that society. Social policies must meet these various agendas while at the same time responding to general social needs. Since the most common interaction of identity, heritage, and culture is found in the urban ethnic community or "the neighborhood," these units must be involved in defining and implementing social policies and programs.

For social programs to reflect the cultural values of the

community, the client population must be involved in the formulation and delivery of social services. The urban political machines in the United States were designed so that community residents controlled service delivery through their votes and through direct contact with their precinct captains. This model can be applied to the design of social service delivery systems organized as social utilities serving neighborhood interests.

In this chapter, McCready suggests a practical model for the formulation of policy and the design of the social service delivery system. Grossman develops the thesis further, showing that in one case—that of health services—the ethnic values of the client population must be considered before adequate service can be provided.

The persistence of ethnic heritages in American society is in direct conflict with the acculturation and assimilation models by which historians and sociologists attempted to show that the influence of immigrants' ethnic heritages declined at some predictable rate through successive generations in America. Ethnic cultural retention is a dynamic force for social identity and is used by individuals and communities at different times for different purposes. Ethnic identification was not established in the homeland, but developed only after the immigrant arrived in the United States. This process of acquiring an ethnic identity is a complex one that sociologists find difficult to explain in detail. Fabian offers this description of the process by which immigrants become ethnics:

> People, while living in their own society, take their culture and identity to a great extent for granted. When, due to some historical circumstances, they leave, this unproblematical nature of reality disappears. But questions of cultural identity arise only when immigrants are asked by the host society, "Who are you?" Significantly, the question, the context within which self-identification is requested, and the evaluation placed upon it are in terms of another culture which in some sense predetermines the answers. Hence the self-identification of the immigrant is not merely a reflection upon the old culture, but a response to a question posed by the host society in terms of its own categories.[1]

[1] Ilona Fabian, *Alternative Perspectives for Studying Ethnicity,* Report to the Ford Foundation (Chicago: Center for the Study of American Pluralism, National Opinion Research Center, January 1973), p. 21.

The response to the question of individual identity is different in different social situations. An ethnic identification may be used by some people and not by others. It may be used in some circumstances and not in others. It may be a way of saying, "My heritage is important to me, is it important to you?"

To say that most people in the United States have come from someplace else is now a truism. Fifty years ago immigrant status was the norm, not the exception. Hyphenated Americanism was both a way of distinguishing oneself from others and of identifying with the larger host culture. This multipurpose ethnic identification was used in many different situations. For example, when questioned by a possible employer, the immigrant could always claim his Americanism to prove his allegiance to the basic national values of hard work and ambition. When queried by his children as to why they should not date someone of another ethnic group, the immigrant could always appeal to his origin to support the values and cultural forces that made out-of-group marriages unacceptable. It could be argued that in order to get along in a pluralistic society it is necessary to have a number of options for social identity. The hyphenated immigrant-American status provided such options.

Three important components of ethnicity are identification, heritage, and culture. Identification is simply the nationality named as the first part of a hyphenated identity. In 1972, 76 percent of the population was able to single out the name of one country from which their ancestors came. In 1973, this figure was 79 percent.[2] Heritage is the more conscious component of ethnic identity in that it represents an interest in the history of an individual's own ethnic group. The diligent search for ancestral roots and the nostalgic interest in the historical past are examples of the new salience of heritage. Culture might be described as the less conscious component of ethnic identity. It consists of attitudes, personality traits, and behavioral patterns associated with a particular ethnic origin. Examples of the cultural component might be the dominance of the mother in the Irish family or the intensity of relationships in the Italian family. There is strong evidence that both of these characteristics existed in the native population long before their arrival on American shores.

[2] *General Social Survey 1972* and *General Social Survey 1973* (Williamstown, Mass.: Roper Public Opinion Research Center, Williams College, 1972 and 1973), pp. 12 and 15, respectively. The question was the same in both surveys: "From what countries or part of the world did your ancestors come?"

These three components interact in different ways at different times in the history of the immigrant group. This has important ramifications for the design of social policies that influence and are influenced by these groups. Ignoring the ethnic components of social reality will only result in the development of additional inadequate and unsuccessful programs for the delivery of social services to the people who most need them.

Perhaps the most common interaction of identity, heritage, and culture is found in the urban ethnic community, or more simply, "the neighborhood." Not all neighborhoods are ethnic communities, and not all ethnics live in neighborhoods. However, the concept of neighborhood provides a useful perspective for discussing the development and impact of social policies. Greeley summarizes the power that comes from the interaction of identity, heritage, and culture:

> When neighborhood loyalty, already something quite primordial, is rein-
> forced by a common religion and sense of common ethnic origins, the
> commitment to the neighborhood can become fierce and passionate
> indeed. Its streets, its markets, its meeting places, its friendships, its
> accepted patterns of behavior, its customs, its divisions, even its factional
> feuds provide a context for life that many of its citizens are most
> reluctant to give up.[3]

Since many of those served by social programs live in such neighborhoods, it is necessary to understand these individuals' reasons for remaining ethnic, or, to put it more sociologically, for "remaining particular" in the face of serious efforts to persuade them to be more "cosmopolitan" or "universal." Ethnicity becomes significant to the individual and to the collectivity when it proves an advantage in dealing with the larger social system. Ethnic identification can provide attractive political, economic, social, and psychological advantages. Ethnicity becomes a way of choosing political leaders one can trust; of competing within a limited economic locus; of forming friendships based on mutual assistance; and of affiliating with the dominant culture without denying those roots that sustain the ego.

However, the neighborhood cannot close itself off from the rest of society without paying an intolerably high price. There are some things smaller communities cannot efficiently do for themselves. It is neither practical nor economically feasible for smaller communities to provide all the services needed by community residents. The crucial

---

[3] Andrew M. Greeley, *Why Can't They Be Like Us?* (New York: E. P. Dutton & Co., 1971), p. 100.

problem for the ethnic community or neighborhood is to make its needs known to the larger society and at the same time to retain some control over the way those needs are met. Nothing can diminish the dignity of a people faster or more ruthlessly than subjecting them to a social program over which they have no control.

It is a demonstrable fact that the quickest way for a group to draw attention to its needs is to become "a social problem." This is also the quickest route to the loss of control over whatever programs are eventually designed to meet those needs. The ethic of pragmatism has dominated many attempts to solve social problems in the United States.

IMPLICATIONS OF ETHNIC DIVERSITY

One of the debilitating characteristics of policy-making oriented toward solving problems is the inability of society to deal with more than one problem at a time. Thus, whichever group demonstrates the greatest problem will receive the lion's share of policy attention. Those groups of predominantly European heritage who inhabit the large cities, particularly in the northeastern quadrant of the United States, have of late not been problem groups; but then neither have they had a part in problem-solving. They can be characterized by their support and willingness to pay for progressive social policies without having a voice in choosing either the problem to be solved or how the solutions are implemented.[4]

This does not mean that the problems addressed, such as racial discrimination, are not critical, but merely that these are not the only problems. Increasingly, citizens described as white European ethnics are becoming fearful that they are being ignored by the policy-making process of society. The American system, which once appeared to work so well, no longer seems responsive to them. A pluralistic system that cannot be attentive to all its groups must be prepared for dissension and division. As long as a group feels that their particular agenda is represented on the larger social agenda, they will generally be cooperative. When they feel their agenda is not being recognized, they are likely to become recalcitrant.

The creation of social policies in a pluralistic society requires two interrelated operations. First, the policy-makers must possess the means

---

[4] Andrew M. Greeley, "Political Attitudes among American White Ethnics," *Public Opinion Quarterly*, 36 (Summer 1972), p. 216.

to accurately read the needs of those for whom policy is intended. Second, the policy must be implemented in such a way as to be useful to the members of the community.

Too often those formulating policy for housing, employment, or education consider these areas only from their own viewpoint. The most direct way to prevent this one-sidedness is to include community members in the initial phase of policy-making, the problem-definition stage, to encourage communication. The second operation, implementing the policy in a usable manner, is more subtle. Even the most well-conceived plan will be a waste of time and money if people cannot derive its intended benefits. If its use implies a threat to personal dignity or self-worth, the service may be of questionable benefit. This has frequently been the case when people have had to deal with large bureaucratic mental health organizations.

CONCEPT OF SOCIAL UTILITIES

Kahn suggests removing the stigma from receiving welfare benefits by adopting the view that these services are "social utilities" in much the same way that electric and telephone services are considered public utilities.[5] Such things as social insurance, public housing, day care centers, and mental health and counseling programs should be considered normal, accepted, regular parts of urban life, which are just as available to the general population as are public utilities. This is an interesting proposal, for it means that people would no longer have to define themselves as problems to obtain assistance in carrying out their social existences.

When a middle-class family needs counseling, they have a number of options. They can seek a private specialist, engage their own doctor, or rely on hospital services and counseling centers; or they can use public agencies with the assurance of receiving some recognition of their status in society. Giordano has shown that working- and lower-class families are not only more reluctant to seek counseling, but are treated disrespectfully when they do.[6] One goal of any future social policy should be to eliminate this bias.

[5] Alfred J. Kahn, *Theory and Practice of Social Planning* (New York: Russell Sage Foundation, 1969), pp. 178–180.

[6] Joseph Giordano, *Ethnicity and Mental Health* (New York: National Project on Ethnic America of the American Jewish Committee, 1973), pp. 30–31.

The true test of any social policy is in the behavioral change it creates in the agencies it governs. It is clear that agency behavior rather than agency attitude makes the crucial difference in the client's view of agency operations.[7] In determining how well social utilities serve urban ethnic groups, it is necessary to measure the extent to which the ethnic group perceives social agencies and their policies as benevolent or threatening. Research has indicated that, in the case of some agencies, the less the agency interferes in the client's life, the more positively the client is apt to view the agency. The less the client sees his caseworker, the more likely he is to be satisfied with agency operations.[8]

White ethnics' perceptions of social welfare agencies and social policy must be set in the context of their general perceptions of the American experience. People of European descent who live in the large metropolitan areas of the United States often seem paradoxical to others. Their world view is a difficult one for cosmopolitan social commentators to understand. They are intensely "American," highly patriotic, and committed to the fundamental goals of the republic. At the same time, they are proud of their own heritage, proud that they came from someplace other than America, and proud of their immigrant origins. They tend to be conservative in a moral and religious sense. Accordingly, they adopt the ideological positions of brotherhood and good will between men of all races. However, they are deeply committed to the values of family, neighborhood, and community, and most are economically marginal. As a result, they are likely to be frightened and threatened by the idea of sudden change in the racial composition of their neighborhoods, which could cost them money and change the context of their lives.

Although morally and religiously conservative, ethnics are liberal on political and social issues.[9] None of the liberal social legislation of the last twenty-five years would have passed federal, state, or local legislatures without strong support from urban ethnic voters. However, appeals to white ethnics' sense of guilt and shame for offenses committed by a majority on a minority are inappropriate and are met initially with silence and later with anger. These ethnics cannot understand why they should be blamed for events that predated their parents' arrival in America.

---

[7] Peter H. Rossi, Richard A. Berk, and Bettye K. Eidison, *The Roots of Urban Discontent* (New York: Wiley-Interscience, 1974), pp. 364–389.

[8] Ibid., p. 383.

[9] Greeley, "Political Attitudes among American White Ethnics." p. 218.

Because of the paradoxical nature of the ethnic's perception of the American experience, it is important that social policies be directed at the appropriate side of the paradox. For example, if community mental health and family counseling are to be made available in a way that ethnic communities can use them, these services should be offered as social utilities through local institutions, such as labor unions, churches, or schools.[10] Economically insecure white ethnics consider counseling services as something they neither need nor can afford. And though their financial position is marginal, white ethnics find it extremely difficult to seek any kind of welfare service. Most have a long history of self-help, a fierce sort of independence, and a reluctance to rely on any large, impersonal social institution. Perhaps the best method of disseminating economic advice and assistance to these groups is through neighborhood banks and savings and loan associations. It would not be difficult to create consumer education and financial management programs that would be available as a public service through such institutions. These are attractive delivery points, primarily because they have already established a nonthreatening presence in the community. One of several comfortable, acceptable institutions such as a parish school or rectory, a hospital, or a food store can become a source of help for coping with the needs of urban life. It is not necessary for an individual to define himself as "needy," or "disadvantaged," or "socially handicapped" to obtain services provided at these informal sources.

SOCIAL POLICY IN NEIGHBORHOODS

The general principle here is that the most efficient delivery of social services, as well as the most efficient feedback into future policy-making, would be attained by a system that utilizes preexisting neighborhood institutions. The advantage of local institutions is their established relation to the identity, heritage, and culture of the people they serve.

The implementation of any given social policy has two broad areas of influence. The policy will have an impact on the groups it is designed to serve and on the service system in which it functions. Social policies have frequently served to increase the polarization between groups in the pluralistic social structure. The administration of welfare services, for example, has divided white ethnics and lower-

[10] Giordano, op. cit., pp. 36–73.

class blacks, even though many of their self-interests are identical. Similarly, many educational policies have divided the black and white populations they were meant to serve. Instead, social policy should serve to decrease polarization between groups in the society.

It is important to realize that cultural subgroups in society often stress the differences among themselves. Policies that promise to resolve the problems of a specific group or that indicate a specific group is the sole possessor of such problems are basically divisive and polarizing. Policies are needed that impress on all groups which of their common needs can be served by governmental agencies, their equal access to these services, and the agencies' goals of depolarization.

The second aspect of the effect of implementing social policy is no less dangerous. Many institutions of higher education have learned a painful lesson in recent years: When the client, in this case the student, is asked to participate in policy deliberations, the manner of arriving at policy decisions changes. Perhaps adopting a social utility perspective toward social services will convince all groups that they have equal rights to those services. This may produce a temporarily uncomfortable situation for the system of service delivery. Any large bureaucracy develops patterned ways of responding to challenges, requests, and demands. Social service agencies and governmental bureaucracies are certainly no exception. A policy that makes the focus of the agency the groups to· be served rather than the service to be delivered will change many of the accepted and comfortable patterns of behavior within the agency. Just as the black population has increasingly demanded that service agencies recognize them as people with a specific heritage and culture, so these agencies will be asked to recognize Polish-American culture, Italian-American culture, and Irish-American culture, among others. An effort must be undertaken to discover the relevant components of each of these cultures. This implies that the value of each of these must be recognized, respected, and treated with dignity.

One method for improving an agency's awareness of diversity is to employ more members of ethnic communities in social service capacities. Analogously, the lack of representation of white ethnics on university faculties has been documented by the Center for the Study of American Pluralism and others.[11] This lack has severely hampered the ability of the academic world to relate to the culture of the ethnic. Although ethnic quotas for social service agencies are

[11] Andrew M. Greeley, "The 'Religious Factor' and Academic Careers—A Final Note," *American Journal of Sociology*, 78 (March 1973), pp. 1247–1255.

not recommended, recruitment policies should encourage ethnic minority students from diverse backgrounds to matriculate in social service programs. Although students need to develop competence in dealing with anticipated problems, they should not have to deny their cultural backgrounds by developing a new set of values. Thus, it is important for the teacher to appreciate the values expressed by the students rather than to try to change them.

An example of intervention at the local level was the War on Poverty of President Lyndon Johnson's Great Society programs. Controversial rhetoric notwithstanding, it was possible to anticipate the accomplishments of these programs. Some were great successes, and some were failures. Some programs promised more than they could deliver, and produced frustration. Others delivered more than they originally promised. The concept of directing national resources to a local problem demands community preparation for the interaction and community participation in the establishment of goals.

The best model of such interaction in an urban environment is the political machine. This term, which has come into disrepute in recent times, was found, in a recent survey, to have positive connotations for the residents of certain sections of Chicago.[12] The term "machine" conjured up images of efficiency and stability. Essential tasks of the political machine are relating services to community needs and channeling those services through community members. Political issues, which might be analogous to the universal goals of social service agencies, are easily translated to community members in terms of their impact on everyday life. The issues are made nonthreatening for each of the component communities in the political structure. For example, racial balance in the schools should not be stressed in a community where "race" is an inflammatory issue because of recent conflicts in the local school. Instead, attention might better be focused on the need for quality education and for justice within the educational system.

The political structure, analogous to the social service system, is manned by community residents who are easily identified by their neighbors. The masterpiece of the urban political machine was the creation of the precinct captain. A few social workers may have become precinct captains and embarked on political careers; but generally social workers are not educated to be precinct captains. Perhaps they should be. The precinct captain provides a service to the people.

---

[12] This survey was privately done for a potential mayoral candidate and is not available for further analysis.

He translates the needs of the community into political issues, and then he translates issues back to the people in terms of their self-interest. Most precinct captains would probably not recognize such an intellectualized and sterile definition of their jobs. They are more likely to describe their work as listening to people's complaints and then trying to get something done about them. The core element of this process is the precinct captains' proximity to the identity, heritage, and culture of the people they serve. The delivery of social services to urban populations should perhaps be modeled after the political machine instead of the corporate bureaucracy.

It is important to understand that machine politics are not the romantically idealized governmental tactics of George Washington Plunkitt, a ward boss in the infamous Tammany Hall machine at the turn of the century.[13] There is certainly corruption in these organizations, and they have faults that need correction. There is no reason, however, why the model has to be discarded because of its problems or because it has not been universally successful. It is, in fact, the best model available at the present time. Many urban political machines have been unsuccessful because they have been unable to attract young people to their organizations. This was not always the case. Young people once entered political organizations because this was a means of upward mobility. It is possible that someday this situation will exist once again. Meanwhile, the machine model can be adopted by social theorists as a way of incorporating community input into the delivery of social services.

The reluctance with which many in positions of forming social policy greet this model indicates their lack of respect for the origins, behavior patterns, and life-styles of many of the people for whom they profess concern. Understanding why the machine model works is to understand and relish the diversity of the groups participating in American society. The machine model of social services proposes that policy-makers understand these different identifications and treat them as useful components of the human personality rather than obstacles to social progress.

In a way, the proposals of several years ago that encouraged the creation of social ombudsmen began to address the right issues. However, there are many ethnic groups in our country for whom the word "ombudsman" is meaningless. The idea of telling an Irishman from the Bronx or a Pole from the northwest side of Chicago whose

---

[13] William L. Riordon, *Plunkitt of Tammany Hall: A Series of Very Plain Talks on Very Practical Politics* (New York: E. P. Dutton & Co., June 1963).

precinct captain is right on the corner to complain to the ombudsman about the lack of garbage collection is questionable, if not humorous. It is important to remember that the precinct captain represents the larger organization. It is this organization that integrates political issues into everyday life and represents everyday life to policy-makers responsible for social services.

One of the main characteristics of a precinct organization is its ability to take individuals from the neighborhood or the community, enable them to understand political specifics without transforming them into politicians, and return them to the neighborhood as political operatives. In other words, the precinct worker who becomes a cosmopolitan and begins to deal with political universals is useless as a precinct worker. Effective community organizers, salesmen, and clergymen understand this. The intellectual exercise required to create social policies that reflect this genius of the precinct model of political organization, without its abuses, will be intense. The reward, however, will be systems that can deliver social services to the populations in need of them, in a way in which these populations can use them.

SUMMARY

Ethnicity is one of the several identities that people use to position themselves in the social system. The hyphenated national identity is a way of entering into the dominant society without abandoning the cultural heritage. Similarly religious identification, sex role divisions, political identification, and other identifications help individuals define themselves within a system.

One of the noticeable characteristics of white ethnics in America is their fear. They are afraid that their heritage is no longer respected by the majority. They are afraid that the rules by which one gains success have changed. The fear of violence in the neighborhood is widespread. The fear of inflation and occupational layoff and the damage they do to a family's economy is increasing daily. The fear of higher taxes, of higher prices, and of the family's losing its ability to live within its means is particularly great among these working-class people. Most of all, they fear for the future of their children. They fear that the values they respect and find useful will not be passed down to them. Too many institutions in society are attacking those values and diluting them. All these fears tend to make the white ethnics an insecure and socially volatile group. Social policies that do not reflect an understanding of these fears and that do not propose a solution to them are doomed to failure.

People of different identities and heritages want respect for their way of life. They do not want the dominant society to adopt their values, but they do want to be heard. The hyphenated identity is treasured for its unique qualities and for preserving a certain world view. A model for the delivery of social services that combines the perspectives of neighborhood social utilities with precinct-style organization preserves and utilizes the hyphenated identity, because it accurately reflects the identity, heritage, and culture of the people requiring the services.

The neighborhood social utility provides resources without threat and disruption. It is a trusted source of help rather than suspected source of surveillance, which many welfare bureaus have become. People can benefit from the utility without relinquishing any of their personal sense of worth and dignity.

The precinct-style organization of the political machine, when applied to the management of a social utility system of service delivery, provides at least three benefits to the members of the ethnic community. First, by stressing the personal contact with representatives of service agencies, it provides security from the fear of interference from impersonal agencies. Second, it provides feedback from the community that can be incorporated into the planning and execution phases of policy-making. And finally, it maintains respect for the community's values through an understanding of them.

Trust is a much used and often maligned word these days, but the intent here is to describe the formation of a community of trust. Neighborhoods have always dealt in trust, but it is novel to have a social service agency move into a neighborhood and partake of, rather than destroy, that existing climate of trust. Trust, in this context, does not imply high moral goals or high moral development. It does mean that people in ethnic neighborhoods know they can trust the machine to be a machine and work the way it says it will. The effect of such a community of trust is to stabilize the fears of a neighborhood and of a group and to develop within them a tolerance for the ambiguities of living in a modern urban society.

New York Segregation: Implications for Social Policy

NATHAN KANTROWITZ

Nathan Kantrowitz, Ph.D., is Professor, Department of Sociology, Kent State University, Kent, Ohio.

EDITORS' COMMENT

Kantrowitz's study on segregation in New York is in certain respects closely related to Norton's "Residential Environment and Black Self-Image." Both observe that segregation in housing remains unchanged despite balanced income levels and open-housing laws, and both point out that current housing policy is ineffective in eliminating racial segregation. The two articles begin with different premises and data, arrive at similar conclusions about the limitations of residential desegregation as a viable policy, and offer different suggestions for social policy.

Analyses of ethnic diversity are frequently attempted without the support of basic research. Although such research does not necessarily provide solutions to social problems, it can be especially useful as a means to an understanding of social phenomena. Kantrowitz's work is such a case. Using an index of dissimilarity, which is a statistical device that shows the population shift necessary to achieve racial or ethnic balance, and the United States Census, Kantrowitz measures segregation in New York City, not only racially, ethnically, and socioeconomically, but also by religion. He concludes that opposition to residential integration with blacks represents not merely a racial phenomenon but is also an intensification of the more general phenomenon of conflict between different ethnic groups.

Residential segregation by social class and by race will not, in Kantrowitz's view, change significantly in this century. Ethnic residential segregation will probably continue as well, but this will not be easily measured because the major immigrant groups will have reached the third generation, at which point the census ceases to record the origin of the grandparents. Kantrowitz is pessimistic that social policy will ever influence residential segregation and states that a balance must be reached between "prohibiting exclusion" and "enforcing diversity." Norton tends to agree and attempts to suggest policies that will maximize the balance.

─────────────

In creating social policies that modify existing patterns of residential segregation, policy-makers must recognize that the determinants of segregation are tenacious, conservative forces that are not likely to be susceptible to planned change. This conclusion is based on findings from a demographic study, conducted between 1967 and 1972 and published in 1973, of ethnic and racial segregation in New York City.[1] The study examined the residential patterns of white ethnics, blacks, and Puerto Ricans.

The statistics used were derived from the 1960 decennial United States Census; analyses of the 1970 census are still under way and did not even begin to be published until 1974. The census simply records

─────────────

[1] Nathan Kantrowitz, *Ethnic and Racial Segregation in the New York Metropolis: Residential Patterns Among White Ethnic Groups, Blacks, and Puerto Ricans* (New York: Praeger, 1973). This book contains a full discussion of the many technical considerations that bear on the study discussed in this essay.

the residential location of each person interviewed.[2] The census bureau routinely asks each respondent about his racial background, but the data on ethnicity are less complete. Only one person in every four enumerated by the census was asked which state or possession of the United States or which foreign country he was born in, as well as the country where his father and his mother were born. Thus, the "foreign-born" were those who reported they were born in some country other than the United States, while the "native-born with foreign or mixed parentage" were those who reported they were born in the United States to one or both parents born abroad. The foreign-born plus the native of foreign or mixed parentage equal this article's demographic "ethnics," the "foreign stock."

A major methodological point concerns the errors in the census enumeration. Generally, the number of people counted twice is trivial, and net population undercounts in the United States are reckoned in terms of a few percentage points. These percentages soar, however, for certain parts of the population. Whites are apparently counted with reasonable accuracy, but the enumeration of the nonwhite population, especially of young-adult nonwhites, may miss as many as one of every five persons. It has been estimated that, as a national average, the 1960 census underenumerated nonwhite males 20 to 24 years of age by 16.8 to 21.2 percent.[3] Naturally, errors in the data for small areas are potentially even larger. For example, the uncounted among young-adult black males in central city slums far exceed the national average. This occurs not for lack of will on the part of the census bureau, but because of the monumental administrative difficulties of enumeration. All such limitations in the data available from the census shape the methodology used here: there is no reason to apply complex statistical devices whose precision far outreaches the quality of data.

Another problem of data concerns the reliability of statistics for small geographical areas generally and of census tract statistics in particular. All these units, whether counties of a state or census tracts of a city, vary greatly in geographical size and shape as well as popu-

[2] U.S. Department of Commerce, Bureau of the Census, *U.S. Census of Population: 1960,* Vol. 1, *Characteristics of the Population,* Part 1, U.S. Summary (Washington, D.C.: U.S. Government Printing Office, 1964), pp. xi–xci.

[3] Jacob S. Siegel and Melvin Zelnic, "An Evaluation of Coverage in the 1960 Census of Population by Techniques of Demographic Analysis and by Composite Methods," in *Proceedings of the Social Statistics Section 1966* (Washington, D.C.: American Statistical Association, 1967), pp. 71–85.

lation size and density. Contiguous areas are likely to have somewhat similar populations, except in limited areas of cities where mansions and tenements stand back-to-back.

The New York metropolitan area, which includes both central city and suburbs, is divided into census tracts. These tracts were once thought to be small homogeneous "natural areas," but they have proved as unreliable for statistical purposes as other small areas. Although the tracts were once designated in such a way as to be homogeneous, a few decades of shifts in boundary lines and land use can alter an area significantly. Still, with all their deficiencies, census tracts are the smallest geographic units that provide appropriately detailed statistics, and they are, on the average, small enough to form individual tiles in the mosaic of the city.

In this study the index of dissimilarity is used to measure segregation. This is the method preferred by Duncan and Duncan and is the most widely accepted measure in research on segregation.[4] It should be emphasized, however, that no segregation index measures real segregation any more than the Intelligence Quotient measures real intelligence or the Consumer Price Index the real cost of living. All such summary statistics are abstractions whose primary use is for comparison and analysis.

The index of dissimilarity compares two populations at a time and measures the proportion of either population that would have to shift to achieve complete similarity of distribution. An index of 0 percent, for example, means that there is no segregation, and one of 100 percent indicates that there is no heterogeneity, or total segregation. Table 1 indicates the computations used to derive the index of dissimilarity for the four census tracts in the adjoining New York commuter villages of Tarrytown and North Tarrytown. The index in this table measures the segregation between Irish and Italian foreign stock using data from the 1960 census.

The sums of the negative and positive differences will be equal, and either equals the index of dissimilarity. This intuitive rationale and simple example only illustrates the index and does not do justice to the extensive literature on segregation indexes. One obvious limitation of the index of dissimilarity is that it is insensitive to the actual numbers of people involved since it converts the numbers to percentages.

Inherent in this method of computing segregation is the question

TABLE 1. INDEX OF DISSIMILARITY FOR IRISH AND ITALIAN RESIDENTS IN FOUR 1960 CENSUS TRACTS IN TARRYTOWN AND NORTH TARRYTOWN, NEW YORK

| Census Tract | Irish | | Italian | | Differences Between Total Irish and Total Italian |
	Number	Percentage of Total Irish	Number	Percentage of Total Italian	
1	337	33.9	342	15.3	+18.6
2	246	24.8	812	36.2	−11.4
3	267	26.9	904	40.3	−13.4
4	143	14.4	183	8.2	+ 6.2
Total	993	100.0	2,241	100.0	Sum of + = 24.8
					Sum of − = 24.8

Source: U.S. Bureau of the Census, 1960 Census of the Population.

of how one determines what values of the index between 0 (no segregation) and 100 (total segregation) constitute "high" and "low" segregation and what magnitude of numerical change can be taken as an indication of an important change in segregation level. In theory, there is no answer to this problem. For example, simply using larger census tracts would automatically change the index. In practice, however, this question can be resolved by considering indexes upward of 70 percent—which is the range commonly found for the segregation between blacks and whites—as "high," indexes of 30 or less as "low," and variations of less than five points as unimportant unless they are otherwise correlated. This judgment is an important one, for unless it is made a basic assumption, it is impossible to judge the literature in the field enough to come to conclusions about the social reality of the statistics.

SEGREGATION IN NEW YORK, 1960

In this study ethnics are defined as European immigrants and their children. The study seeks to ascertain the degree of segregation between such religious groups as Jews and Catholics and also that between specific nationality groups of the same religious background, Irish Catholics and Italian Catholics, for example. These questions are asked not only for their particular interest but also for the light they may shed on the question of racial segregation. That is, is opposition to integration with blacks primarily a racial phenomenon? The conclusions here differ from those of scholars who believe segregation among European ethnic groups is a trivial and declining phenomenon. On the contrary, it appears that separatism in New York is a strong force well into the second generation and that segregation by race is but an intensification of the interethnic phenomenon.

Social Class. The next set of questions involves segregation among social classes or, in terms of the data, among families according to 1959 income. Here, for convenience in summarizing, only the rich and the poor, whites and blacks are considered. Two kinds of questions evolve. The first concerns segregation within a particular race. Are rich blacks as segregated from their own poor as rich whites are from theirs? Considering the discrimination of the housing market, it might be expected that although there are residential differences between rich and poor blacks, they would be more muted than among whites. Surprisingly, this is not so. Rich blacks are just as segregated from their own poor. This leads to the conclusion that the desire to separate themselves from their own poor is so strong that it motivates middle-class blacks to surmount obstacles of the housing market.

The second question concerning social class segregation involves the effect money has on interracial segregation. For example, one might expect that richer blacks and whites are more integrated than poorer whites and blacks. This is a more direct version of the statement commonly seen in the literature that social class or economics "explains" or accounts for only a limited amount of segregation; that is, poor blacks are segregated from middle-class whites in part just because they are poor. But the data dispute this, for economics appears to explain nothing among economic equals. Moreover, economics appears equally limited in explaining what occurs among the economically disparate. For example, richer blacks are no less segregated from poorer whites than are poorer blacks. Thus, social class explains little about residential patterns; race and, in a limited way, ethnicity, explain much.

Population Change. New York's urban history involves population succession, or the replacement of non-Puerto Rican whites (or "other-whites") by blacks and Puerto Ricans. Although other-white population shifts may often have involved the building of new housing that allowed the ethnic groups to sort themselves out with little conflict, the black and Puerto Rican migrations came later when little inner-city land was available. The poor usually can afford only older housing discarded by stable working or middle classes. Although the evidence is quite limited, this study's findings for blacks and other-whites in New York City corroborate those of Tauber and Tauber for other cities: black movement into other-white areas initially follows social class characteristics.[5] Upper-class blacks move into middle-class other-white areas; only afterwards do lower-class blacks follow. However, no such pattern appears among Puerto Ricans. Further studies of the decade between 1960 and 1970 will help in substantially revising theories of change in urban areas.[6]

SEGREGATION BY ETHNICITY

In assessing the evidence of whether there has been a decline in ethnic segregation, the segregation of specific ethnic groups from one another, such as Irish from Italian, is the central concern. The major relevant study is Lieberson's *Ethnic Patterns in American Cities.*[7] Lieberson's analysis of segregation from 1910 to 1950 in ten northeastern and midwestern central cities—with suburbs excluded from the study— found convincing evidence of a process of assimilation among the foreign-born. The segregation of immigrant groups from one another as well as from all native whites consistently declined as their socio-economic status rose.

As part of his study, Lieberson looked at the segregation of foreign-born whites by country of birth in city wards between 1910 and 1920 and in census tracts between 1930 and 1950. For each of the ten cities, he calculated the segregation index of each ethnic group, so that he derived perhaps fifty indexes per city for such comparisons as Irish with Italian, German with Irish, and Italian with Russian. There was a small decline in the unweighted average of the indexes, city by city. For example, Cleveland's average decreased, by wards, from 50.6 in 1910 to 43.5 in 1920; by census tracts, from 60.8 in 1930 to 54.3 in 1950. In the remaining nine cities, the declines were similarly consistent and small.

The decline of approximately five points between 1930 and 1950

[5] Karl E. Tauber and Alma F. Tauber, *Negroes in Cities.* (Chicago: Aldine Publishing Co., 1965).

[6] For an early contribution to this analysis, *see* Terry J. Rosenberg and Robert W. Lake, "Toward a Revised Model of Residential Segregation: Puerto Ricans in New York, 1960–1970," *American Journal of Sociology,* 18 (March 1976), pp. 1142–1150.

[7] Stanley Lieberson, *Ethnic Patterns in American Cities* (New York: Free Press of Glencoe, 1963).

in the average of segregation indexes is not impressive when one realizes that it was wrought by depression, war, the maturation of a new generation, a postwar expansion of settled areas within and beyond the cities' legal boundaries, and the widespread possession of automobiles and telephones as possible supplements or substitutes for residential propinquity. One should not confuse direction (downward, as Lieberson shows) with an actual drop in level (minimal, as demonstrated in this study).

The decline in average index continued to be consistent but small when Lieberson made the common distinction between the "old" immigrants, those foreign-born from northern Europe whose greatest immigration wave preceded the final quarter of the nineteenth century, and the "new" immigrants, more recent arrivals from southern and central Europe. The segregation indexes for Cleveland between 1930 and 1950 reflect real differences between and among various European ethnic groups. However, these consistent but small declines indicate the existence of relatively stable immigrant enclaves.

New York, 1960. The European ethnic populations, whether "old" stock (82.7) or "new" (80.9), are almost equally segregated from blacks. An equivalent ethnic segregation appears to occur with the Puerto Ricans, again whether their segregation from the "old" (81.6) or "new" (77.2) European stock is considered. It appears that the appreciably lower (63.8) segregation between blacks and Puerto Ricans stems in large measure from the recent date of both their migrations to New York City: the greatest number of European migrants came prior to World War I; most black migrants came since World War I; and most Puerto Ricans since World War II.

Whatever reasons are posited for the extensive segregation between European ethnic groups and blacks or Puerto Ricans, it can be assumed that a guide to the lower bounds or minimum levels of these segregations will be found in the segregation among European ethnicities. The average level of segregation (41.1) among northern Europeans in the New York Standard Metropolitan Statistical Area is virtually identical to that among southern Europeans (38.9). But the average segregation between northern and southern Europeans is markedly higher (51.6). It is reasonable to consider this average index of 51.6 as the lower boundary for 1960 segregation of foreign stock from blacks or Puerto Ricans. In effect, nearly forty years after the end of large-scale European migration, a segregation index number encompassing the migrants and, in particular, their children in a highly suburbanized metropolis, indicates that, on the average, 51.6

percent of the population of southern European origin would have to be redistributed in order to achieve full integration with the northern European population. Consequently, we expect that any given black-white segregation index number will exceed this base. But whatever judgment one makes, it is likely that any reduction of racial segregation will involve the reduction, not of segregation simply between blacks and whites, but rather of blacks and specific white ethnic populations, a task made difficult by the high level in interethnic segregation. Thus, if blacks were white, their segregation levels would be no less than the ethnic 51.6. Making allowances for the recency of migration, the percentage figure for the segregation index would be no less than the lower 60s.

Some of the New York patterns illustrated in Table 2 may not be found in every metropolitan area in the United States. But it appears that the 1960 ethnic segregation patterns of the New York metropolis are similar to those of Chicago and most other northeastern and midwestern cities. These ethnic segregation index numbers reflect a social reality that will probably exist for the rest of this century. Certainly for the present, the strong prejudice against blacks by whites only compounds an existing separation, for if Protestant Norwegians hesitate to integrate with Protestant Swedes, and Catholic Italians with Catholic Irish, then these groups are even less likely to accept black neighbors.

SEGREGATION BY SOCIAL CLASS

It is reasonable to assume that money buys some acceptance for otherwise low status people and that the moneyed classes of any ethnic or racial origin wish some separation from the poor, their own included. Thus, if it were possible statistically to distinguish the rich from the poor among Irish and Italian Catholics, the upper classes of these ethnic groups would likely be found to be less segregated from one another than their overall segregation levels indicate. Indeed, it is possible that an appreciable part of the overall separation between Irish and Italian Catholics stems from the fact that the Irish may be an overall higher social class than the Italians. This possibility cannot be investigated, however, since no statistics on social class for these ethnic groups by census tract are available. On the other hand, sufficiently detailed statistics are available to investigate these questions as they apply to the nation's poorest populations, the blacks and Puerto Ricans.

TABLE 2. INDEXES OF 1960 RESIDENTIAL SEGREGATION BETWEEN SELECTED ETHNICITIES IN THE NEW YORK STANDARD METROPOLITAN STATISTICAL AREA [a]

	United Kingdom	Ireland	Norway	Sweden	Germany	Poland	Czecho-slovakia	Austria	Hungary	USSR	Italy	Negro	Puerto Rico
United Kingdom													
Ireland	28.1												
Norway	51.4	58.7											
Sweden	31.8	41.3	45.8										
Germany	25.6	33.3	56.4	38.2									
Poland	45.0	51.7	67.9	57.9	47.9								
Czechoslovakia	39.5	44.5	65.6	51.1	39.5	41.7							
Austria	40.2	47.1	68.0	54.2	40.4	20.3	39.9						
Hungary	39.1	44.2	68.3	52.9	38.7	31.3	33.9	24.7					
USSR	50.2	57.1	72.9	62.2	52.1	20.0	49.0	19.0	32.7				
Italy	44.9	48.0	60.2	51.9	45.6	52.7	51.6	53.0	53.9	60.5			
Negro	80.3	80.3	88.4	83.7	80.6	79.7	81.9	81.1	80.4	81.8	80.5		
Puerto Rico	79.8	76.5	88.2	83.9	79.7	75.5	78.6	76.6	76.3	78.1	77.8	63.8	

Source: U.S. Bureau of the Census, 1960 Census of Population.

[a] Ethnicities are defined as the foreign stock (foreign born plus native born with one or both parents foreign born.) *Negro* is a racial category defined by the Census Bureau.

Although the New York study conducted by the author contrasts nonwhites and Puerto Ricans with the remaining population of non-Puerto Rican whites, social class segregation, for the sake of clarity, shall be summarized simply in terms of blacks and whites, rich and poor. Thus, the four groups that will be dealt with are rich blacks, poor blacks, rich whites, and poor whites. For each of these groups there are three questions that need to be considered:

1. Within a racial group, how much do the rich separate themselves from their own poor?

2. How does the degree of segregation between blacks and whites of the same level of wealth compare to the average degree of segregation between all whites and blacks?

3. Are blacks and whites of dissimilar levels of wealth more segregated than whites and blacks on the average?

On the first question, there is an extensive body of scholarship indicating nationally that money buys housing choices, and that the rich of a racial group do segregate themselves from their own poor. Schnore's data for the New York metropolis confirms this finding.[8] Given the discrimination in the housing market, it could be expected that rich blacks would be less segregated from their own poor than rich whites because the blacks would have more difficulty translating their desires into practice.

The results of this study, however, indicate the opposite: rich blacks are as segregated from poor blacks as rich whites are from poor whites. One could even argue that they are slightly more segregated. There may be two reasons for this. Either there is little discrimination in the housing market, which is most unlikely, or else rich blacks are strongly motivated to surmount the existing housing market obstacles. Although the data do not differentiate between these two reasons, it is reasonable to conclude that the motivations of the rich, whether black or white, are similar.

The second and third questions raise the issue of what happens to racial segregation when money is involved. The evidence here leads to the conclusion that money does not decrease segregation. Calculating the segregation levels between poor blacks and poor whites and between rich blacks and rich whites shows that the segregation remains high in both cases. Thus, increasing the incomes of blacks, whatever its other benefits, does not substantially affect integration between wealthier blacks and whites.

In answer to the third question, the actual levels of segregation

---

[8] Leo F. Schnore, *The Urban Scene* (New York: The Free Press, 1965).

between disparate groups of rich blacks and poor whites, as well as between poor blacks and rich whites, were calculated. Although the issue here is more complicated, the findings indicate that disparate increase creates no striking shifts in segregation levels. Rich blacks do not use their greater housing flexibility to integrate with poorer whites who have more limited options.

In summary, then, this study, using a simple investigation of detailed statistics, concludes that race tends to determine the limited role of economics. Extending this conclusion to Puerto Ricans, it appears that rich Puerto Ricans are as segregated from poor Puerto Ricans as rich non-Puerto Rican whites or nonwhites are from their poor. There was no pattern to indicate that higher incomes impel wealthier Puerto Ricans to integrate with nonwhites or non-Puerto Rican whites of any income class.

RESIDENTIAL SEGREGATION AND PUBLIC POLICY

New York's ethnic separation appears to have a continuity that has withstood the shocks of suburbanization and prosperity. Indeed, as the residential patterns for New York's blacks and Puerto Ricans indicate, higher incomes do not lead to integration between races.

If the present study's interpretation of residential segregation in New York has any relevance to other cities, it appears to suggest that social class segregation is strong and that the ties of European ethnicity and religion still strongly motivate residential segregation. The importance and persistence of social class segregation is not surprising, for this appears to be a nearly universal phenomenon in large industrial or commercial urban areas.

Moreover, it can be anticipated that, when the statistics have been analyzed, the 1970 census will show that social class segregation remains as strong in New York as it was in 1960. In fact, the 1960 levels may be duplicated throughout this century. This is a somewhat mechanical projection based on the common prevalence of social class segregation in other cities and societies. It reflects an assumption that attempts to modify this social norm by such governmental efforts as zoning changes will fail. Some areas may be changed in their class composition from middle to lower class, but it is unlikely that middle- and lower-class populations will be any more intermingled than they are now.

Although ethnic segregation may show some decline in the 1970 census, any such decline will probably be small. There appears to be a limit to the extent to which any group will tolerate its own dispersion. Even liberal, middle-class suburban Jews will not want integration to proceed to the point that the population base of their synagogue is imperiled. In 1960, an average of 51.6 percent of the foreign stock would have had to be redistributed to achieve ethnic integration. This percentage declined little in the next decade; the figure for 1970 was 44.8 percent.[9] Beyond the year 1970 the census data will probably be lacking because of the census bureau's practice of not asking for the nationality of grandparents. In 1970, it was nearly half a century since the end of large-scale immigration into the United States, and the survivors of these earlier generations had dwindled. By 1980, the numbers will be quite small. The second generation will remain large until the end of the century, but the availability of ethnic statistics will decline.

The decline in ethnic separatism will probably depend on the intangibles of future interests and events. Glazer and Moynihan's belief was that ethnic groups are also interest groups with identities forged in part by their place in economic and social organizations.[10] That is, to speak of Italians in New York City is, in part, to speak of Sanitation Department employees, and to speak of Jews is to consider, in part, the children of Russian or Polish immigrant Jews who are schoolteachers. The viability of ethnic groups as interest groups is shaped by events no one can foretell. For example, the current glorification in films of Italian criminals and the challenges by blacks and Puerto Ricans to Jews for teaching jobs will help shape the identity of Italian and Jewish groups. As that identity is reinforced or eroded, so will be the viability of the residential enclaves that identification supports.

It is probable that the evidence in the 1970 census will indicate that the levels of segregation between blacks or Puerto Ricans and white ethnic groups and between blacks and Puerto Ricans were possibly even higher then than in the 1960 census. This may be attributed to several causes: continued ethnic separation, discrimination against the newest of newcomers, the heightened conflicts between interest groups that occurred during the 1960s, and the continued large-scale migration into the city of the black population during the decade between 1960 and 1970. Only when migration diminishes will there be an opportunity for an appreciably lessened segregation. But even

[9] Sharon E. Bleda, "Bases of Ethnic Residential Segregation." Paper presented at the annual meeting of the American Sociological Association, 1975.

[10] Nathan Glazer and Daniel Moynihan, *Beyond the Melting Pot* (Cambridge, Mass.: The MIT Press, 1963).

if migration were to decline immediately, it could not be anticipated that any large changes would be found during this century.

It seems clear, both from the Tauber and Tauber 1965 study and from Kantrowitz's 1973 study, that among blacks the upper classes were the first to move into white areas and were followed by their own lower classes.[11] However, the evidence about the pattern of "other-white" and Puerto Rican movement is inconclusive. Also, a geographic study highlights the already noticeable fact that each territorial settlement of nonwhites or Puerto Ricans becomes a social class segment of the citywide population.[12] Thus, in 1960 black Harlem was by and large a lower-class segment of New York's black population, whereas St. Albans in Queens was largely a richer one. The social class characteristics of the populations of each of these areas are likely to remain the same for the rest of this century. Socially mobile blacks will probably leave Harlem or Bedford-Stuyvesant to move to Queens.

Finally, it is apparent that the conclusions presented here carry pessimistic implications for the hope that public policies will influence residential segregation between rich and poor and between ethnic or racial populations. The failure of these public policies will in turn affect other policies. Thus, changing educational systems by busing children out of their local areas or by upgrading slum schools may not be viable policies. But accomplishing these objectives in education by means of residential desegregation—either by government action or by relying on personal, individual decisions—is not likely. This research thus indicates that policy-makers must recognize the tenacity with which ethnic communities resist residential change. It is here, however, that the guidance of research ends; for in specific situations a balance must be reached between "prohibiting exclusion" and "enforcing diversity."

[11] Tauber and Tauber, op. cit.; and Kantrowitz, op. cit.

[12] Nathan Kantrowitz, *Negro and Puerto Rican Populations of New York in the Twentieth Century* (New York: American Geographical Society, 1969).

part two

ETHNIC IDENTITY

Personality Development and Ethnic Identity

J. GARY MAY, MD

J. Gary May, MD, is Director, Adolescent Psychiatry Program, University of Colorado Medical Center at Denver.

EDITORS' COMMENT

The test of social policy lies in how it affects the individual. In America, the individual must learn to live in a pluralistic society, where the ability to interact with persons of different ethnic and racial groups is essential. However, since the model of a homogeneous society in which all are assimilated has been perpetuated, ethnic and racial identity has rarely been taken into account in creating models of childhood development that have implications for social policy.

The emotional consequences of prejudice and discrimination are rooted in childhood. The tendency to overvalue an adult perspective on environment and culture underemphasizes the experience of growing up. May stresses the importance of early interactions within the family and the role these experiences play in establishing the basis of self-esteem and identity.

The development of ethnic consciousness and ethnic identity is, as Cafferty and Chestang demonstrate, vital for minority group children, and an understanding of ethnicity is important to all children in their relationships with others.

Simply coping with the effects of racism is not enough. Social planning to decrease its impact or to modify the experience of an already prejudiced people is important, but the ultimate question is whether racism can be prevented.

In considering prevention, it is necessary to examine the origins of prejudicial feelings in human beings. If it is phylogenetic, prejudice is an unalterable component of the human personality. If it is not, perhaps prejudice is the product of environmental interpersonal experiences beginning in childhood. Similarly, prejudice may be viewed as the realization of one of man's negative propensities, a basic flaw in the design of mankind, perhaps destined to be reflected forever in human history where it is translated into war, violence, aggression, and hate.

The quest for an understanding of the nature of personality and the causes of behavior has acquired an increasingly scientific basis over the last seventy years. Several major conclusions can be offered as a result of that effort. Personality is a product of the developmental experience, that is, of a combination of genetic influences and life-experiences that have an impact on the character of the adult. Many of the foundation blocks of personality are laid early in childhood. On this foundation will rest the later experiences associated with the development of a sense of self, a feeling of personal identity, and a sense of connection with one's own origins, roots, family, pigmentation, body build, religious origins, social history, and personal worth. All these will be reflected in a sense of identity.

Of overwhelming importance to the individual is his sense of ethnic identity, which begins in early childhood and becomes increasingly poignant. Some resolution of one's ethnicity is necessary in a society filled with individuals who are not only unsure of how they feel about those of different ethnic origins but have yet to resolve their own sense of ethnic identity.

If there is a great lesson that has been learned in the last seventy years of studying human behavior, it is that people behave as society expects them to behave. This is a simple statement of a complex collection of forces, but the corollary pertinent here is apparent none-theless: If we examine the expectations of a racist society about an ethnic group—the expectations, for example, of social incompetence, aggression, or passivity—then that behavior will occur often enough to "confirm" the substance of the prejudice. It is a monumental task for a child to overcome the forces of social expectation through the development of his own ethnic identity.

FORMATION OF ETHNIC IDENTITY

Identity and its formation are made more complex by the movement, progress, and influence of multiple factors through time. A person, in a sense, is handed family and ethnic environment at birth. His sense of self, who he is, will then be determined by a complex interaction of forces that with age will vary in their impact and importance. Adults, having forgotten what it was like to be a child, tend to emphasize the adult experience of environment and culture, and un-deremphasize the experience of growing up.

That temperament is formed *in utero* is the finding of several studies. One suggests that hormonal activity associated with the atti-tudes and feelings of the mother may begin to "tune" the fetus to an emotional set or propensity that will prompt the child to respond to stimuli with specific emotional responses.[1] Although the impact of intrauterine experience remains controversial, there is increasing evi-dence that temperamental differences assume importance even at birth. Chess hypothesizes that "infants do not experience the world in iden-tical terms. Instead they show marked differences in various areas of behavior such as perceptual response, sensory threshold, autonomic response patterns, motility, and sleeping and feeding patterns."[2] Tem-perament includes those characteristics that are independent of the content of any behavior and encompasses adaptability, energy level, mood, ability to focus attention, and the tempo of the child. Different temperamental styles may influence how an infant, from birth, fits into his particular family.

With birth the process of developing security and trust begins.

[1] *See*, for example, Paul H. Mussen, John J. Conger, Jerome Kagan, *Child Development and Personality* (4th ed.; New York: Harper & Row, 1974), pp. 115–16.

[2] Stella Chess, *An Introduction to Child Psychiatry* (2nd ed.; New York: Grune & Stratton, 1969), p. 19.

If it is successfully completed, the result will be an individual who feels good about himself and comfortable with those around him. If this process of adaptation is less than successful, the individual will be anxious, suspicious, and unsure of himself and his identity. These beginning developmental experiences predate the child's awareness of ethnic identity but are influenced by his parents' sense of their own identities. If they remain anxious, unsure, and insecure, these will be expressed in their relationship with the child and will perpetuate the problems they experienced while growing up. It is important to remember that "temperament is not immutable. Like any other characteristic of the organism, its features can undergo a developmental course that will be significantly altered by environmental circumstances." [3]

The biological aspects of temperament are operational at birth. However, before the child can begin to establish a sense of identity, he must first develop a sense of self. One of the early stages in the process of becoming aware of self occurs at 8 months when the baby develops what Spitz has called "stranger anxiety." [4] Before then, the child cannot distinguish himself from his mother. At about 8 months the mental apparatus is developed enough for the baby to see his mother, remember her face, compare it to other faces, and, if they do not match hers, become upset. He begins to separate and categorize individuals according to distinctive physical characteristics.

Later the child learns to walk and talk, and begins to think. He also begins, at about 18 months, to learn that some things are "good" or "bad," "clean" or "dirty," "nice" or "not nice." He also learns shame as his mother shows displeasure when he is "bad," "dirty," or "not nice." The child, seeking to avoid feelings of shame, displaces the blame, act, or feeling on someone or something outside himself— "the chair tripped me" or "the cat messed up the room." This sets the stage for later utilization of the same mechanisms of differentiation and displacement as precursors of prejudice.

ETHNIC AND RACIAL AWARENESS IN YOUNG CHILDREN

To learn how children develop a sense of race, Goodman studied racial awareness in 103 4-year-old children, 57 of whom were "Negroes" by social definition, that is, by marked physical variation such as

[3] Ibid., p. 20.

[4] René A. Spitz, *The First Year of Life* (New York: International Universities Press, 1965), p. 150.

pigment or hair.[5] The 4-year-old has a strong sense of self and of others. Finding that about one-fourth of the children in her study had firmly entrenched race-related values, Goodman remarked: "It is shocking to find these 4-year-olds, particularly white ones, show unmistakable signs of the onset of racial bigotry."

Eighty-five percent of the children studied had medium-to-high awareness of race. In the black group, many of the children were distressingly direct in their equation of black with bad or dirty. One black child saw whites as "prettier" and "nicer." The brown doll was "the dirty one." Black girls were aware of lighter siblings, and one asked her mother when she would be lighter too. The word "dirty" was frequently used and often in relation to blackness.

This equation of "dirty" or "not nice" with darker color has been a particularly perplexing and disturbing aspect of children's awareness of race. It impinges on the child of darker pigmentation in his development of self-image. As a child becomes conscious of his own pigmentation, hair, and facial characteristics, he becomes aware of his origins, his appearance, and the background of his family. One of the major tasks of childhood is for that awareness to be associated with a positive, meaningful sense of self.

Thus, the issue becomes one of helping a child develop a sense of positive personal identity, which includes pride in who he is, what he looks like, his ethnic roots, and how he acts. How the child feels about his body represents an important aspect of the development of racial prejudice. The body, after all, is the conveyor of racial characteristics. The body's color, conformation, and characteristics are the focus of reactions. This fact seems to be omitted from many discussions of prejudice and ethnicity in favor of emphasis on psychology and attitudes, cultures and societies, groups and histories.

The psychoanalyst Kubie advances the proposition that prejudice has three roots in early human development.[6] The first is "the child's oscillation between a secret guilty pride in his body and hidden feelings of profound aversion towards his body." The second is the child's inability to conceive of himself as ever becoming an adult "equal in size and strength to those giants who surround him." The third is "inability to accept on all psychological levels the anatomical difference between the sexes."

[5] Mary Ellen Goodman, *Race Awareness in Young Children* (New York: Macmillan Co., 1952), p. 245.

[6] Lawrence S. Kubie, "The Ontogeny of Racial Prejudice," *Journal of Nervous and Mental Diseases,* 141 (September 1965), pp. 265–73.

The child oscillates between the hate of his own appearance and the projection of that hate onto others. To secretly love who you are, or more specifically your body, is contrasted at other times with considerable anxiety and aversion to that same body. It keeps changing and altering itself. He is small and insignificant in relation to adults. His body is not like that of at least half the world (the other sex); and he alternates between feeling superior and inferior as a result. The focus on the other person as the alien, as being different and therefore of dirty color or sex, then externalizes the conflict as the alien becomes the "bad" or "dirty" recapitulation of one's own body. Kubie concludes, "The challenge of prejudice includes the challenge to find out how to teach the child wise restraints and the ability to postpone gratification in the use of his body but without making him hate his body!" [7]

Whereas the psychological and sociological literature previously focused on prejudice instead of ethnic identity, current emphasis is on the ethnic pride of the individual—the ability to be proud of who you are, where you came from, what your family represents, with a personal sense of identity, hopefully encouraged and not transmuted by society at large. This is an identity that has its origins in childhood and its development fostered by the experience of relationships in a culture that understands and encourages the child to be whoever he is.

Allport, quoting the study by Harris et al., emphasized how a child learns to be prejudiced. "A home that is suppressive, harsh or critical—where the parents' word is law—is more likely to prepare the groundwork for group prejudice." [8] According to Allport, a child brought up in a home where he feels secure and loved and not subjected to "display of parental power" will be predisposed to tolerance.[9] This corresponds to the findings of Ackerman and Jahoda regarding antisemitism—prejudiced people come from homes characterized by quarreling, violence, divorce, and lack of affection between parents.[10] In Allport's words, "Prejudice may not be taught by the parent but was caught by the child from an infected atmosphere." [11]

---

[7] Ibid., p. 272.

[8] Gordon W. Allport, *The Nature of Prejudice* (New York: Doubleday & Co., 1954), p. 284.

[9] Ibid., p. 283.

[10] Nathan W. Ackerman and Marie Jahoda, *Antisemitism and Emotional Disorder* (New York: Harper & Bros., 1950).

[11] Allport, op. cit., p. 285.

The same factors are also vital to the child's view of himself. Fear of the stranger plays an important role in prejudice. In some ways, at varying times in their lives, all children see themselves as strange. As children grow, they are different today from what they were yesterday. They are filled with new feelings, reside in a new and growing body, and feel alien to themselves. This strangeness is overcome by displacing it onto others who are obviously different.

THE SCHOOL-AGE CHILD

The child grows and rapidly reaches an age when he will enter school. At that time, particularly if he has not had preschool experience, he will face a test of his identity. He will be exposed, perhaps for the first time, to children with characteristics and backgrounds different from his own. Unfortunately, these new experiences will be accompanied by intense, competitive demands and considerable stress on his previously established sense of identity. In school he often is forced to defend who he is and respond to any small variation between himself and the other children. From this point, a great deal of the child's sense of identity will be tested and developed by group expectations. In a sense, every child feels alone, separate, and fearful. He is afraid others will sense the things about him that he feels are different or inadequate. Each child, as a separate individual, must come to terms with himself, and his origins, his appearance, and his uniqueness.

The problems of the minority child in the school situation are enormous. Every child is concerned with his ability to meet the new demands of school, with his popularity among his peers, and with acceptance by his teachers. He enters the school situation not knowing what to expect, unsure of what demands will be placed on him. If he is a minority child, he may be surrounded by members of another race and a different socioeconomic level.

The purpose of school has been to help children master various tasks and situations. One must hope that the school is sensitive to and operates with concern for the feelings of the child. Properly handled, the experience of exposure to different children can become an important source of mastery and strength. If the school is not adequate to the task or is insensitive to the feelings of the child, this experience can destroy a child's sense of self, alienate him from his own ethnicity, fragment him from his family, and render him an alien within his own body. In *The Me Nobody Knows,* Joseph poignantly reflects the alienation and depression of poor and minority children. A summary of that feeling might be characterized by the comment of Arthur Jackson, age 15, who wrote, "I have felt lonely, forgotten, or even left out, set apart from the rest of the world. I never wanted out, if anything I wanted in." [12]

It is often difficult, if not impossible, for a minority child to find appropriate objects for positive identification in school material. Only recently have schools begun to use readers and primers that portrayed minority children. In 1968, Waite examined a set of multicultural, first-grade reading texts introduced in 1962 by the Detroit school system. Whereas prior to 1962, "Negro" characters were excluded from American primers, these new texts portrayed basically middle-class black and white families. In 1964 Hispanic characters were added to the series.[13]

Any consideration of visual and cognitive communication raises the question of language. Officially using more than one language in a school system can be an expression of valuing ethnic diversity and a reflection of the advantages of cultural pluralism. American society has overemphasized the importance of integration and equality at the expense of the non-English-speaking child's self-image, especially that of the Hispanic child. The price has been a failure to communicate effectively with many of these children. To the child who speaks a language other than English or whose parents speak another language, language is an important representation of his ethnic identity. He discovers how the world responds to him as he enters school and sees what is thought of his language.

Karnes, Teska, and Hodgins compared techniques to facilitate intellectual and language development in 4-year-old disadvantaged children and concluded that "the distinguishing characteristic of the [most effective] program was the tying of verbalization to motor sensory performance." [14] To insist that a child from a foreign language background should learn to speak English and be exposed in preschool

[12] Stephen M. Joseph, *The Me Nobody Knows* (New York: Avon Books, 1969), p. 36.

[13] Richard R. Waite, "Some Character Types in Negro Primers: A Psychoanalytic Study." Paper presented at the Denver Psychoanalytic Society, February 1968.

[14] Merle B. Karnes, James A. Teska, and Audrey S. Hodgins, "The Effects of Four Programs of Classroom Intervention on Intellectual and Language Development of Four-Year-Old Disadvantaged Children," *American Journal of Orthopsychiatry*, 40 (January 1970), p. 75.

only to English may well result in establishing in that child a solid and easily perpetuated propensity to developmental failure. Little children must be taught predominantly in their own language.

UNDERSTANDING IDENTITY FORMATION

Perhaps the most important compilation of the current understanding of identity comes from Erikson. In his schema delineating the various stages of the life cycle, Erikson identifies adolescence as the vital period in which the identity takes shape against possible "role diffusion." [15] Adolescence is the time when identity is the overriding psychological issue. The adolescent must consolidate his social role in the face of dramatic physical changes. He must forsake and redevelop his models, idols, and ideals. Unlike the child, he will not respond to simple praise and reassurance but requires substantive recognition of real accomplishment. If this process fails, the result is, in Erikson's terms, "identity diffusion" with strong doubts of "one's ethnic and sexual identity." [16]

This threat of identity diffusion thus becomes the backdrop against which the minority youth's struggle for identity must be understood. The choices that the culture offers this individual are usually restrictive and nonindividualistic, and they leave him with a lasting conflict between those negative expectations and his awareness of himself as an individual. That this society has in some ways found the black person more acceptable as the aggressive, sadistic rapist than as the complex, effective, well-to-do executive, poet, or professor suggests the general destructiveness of the culture's expectations for this group.

In American culture the oppressive nature of group identification and expectation are readily apparent: an "American" is this, a "black" is that, everyone is "middle class," some things (school, milk, and money, for example) are good for everyone. This is what Erikson calls caricature, a form of identity fragmentation. He puts it this way:

> Tired of this caricature, the colored individual often retires into hypochondriac invalidism as a condition which represents an analogy to the

[15] Erik H. Erikson, *Identity and the Life Cycle* (New York: International Universities Press, 1959), p. 90.
[16] Ibid.

ego-space-time of defined restriction in the South: a neurotic regression to the ego identity of the slave.[17]

Fortunately, a new set of ethnic models has been developing within minority cultures. The prominence in Bennett's work of unusual, complex, exciting, and important individuals who were black, the development of the concept of "Chicano" and "La Raza" in the Hispanic community, and the reawakening of the majority culture to the special contribution of the rich and varied American Indian culture may begin to undo the strict stereotyped expectations that impinge upon the minority child's sense of self.

THE PSYCHOSOCIAL DIMENSION OF IDENTITY

Every young person, regardless of ethnic background, must face a basic conflict between group identification and the sense of being an individual. The resolution depends in part on the ability to identify with several groups—such as the family, an ethnic group, and one's peers—and still define one's self as a total individual whose group identifications are part, but not the entirety, of the total self. The outcome, a sense of personal identity,

> . . . is based on two simultaneous observations: the immediate perception of one's selfsameness and continuity in time; and the simultaneous perception of the fact that others recognize one's sense of sameness and continuity.[18]

The bicultural adolescent must look for a way to integrate several identity expectations. He may be placed in a disruptive psychological situation that forces him to assume a role that conforms to the expectations of the dominant group but that is socially maladaptive because it derives from the negative stereotype of his racial group. As Derbyshire puts it, "Forced acculturation of minorities by the dominant group may be dysfunctional for adequate and accurate integration of dominant value orientations and behavior."[19] In his study of the identity problems of adolescent Mexican-Americans, Derbyshire concludes that pride in one's cultural heritage is essential to

[17] Ibid., p. 38.

[18] Ibid., p. 23.

[19] Robert L. Derbyshire, "Adolescent Identity Crisis in Urban Mexican Americans in East Los Angeles," in Eugene B. Brody, ed., *Minority Group Adolescents in the United States* (Baltimore: Williams & Wilkins, 1968), p. 108.

reducing the crisis of adolescent identity and resolving role-conflict. The adolescent must accept and be comfortable with all that he is. Socially, youths must be encouraged to be all they can be and not be "put down," restricted, or forced to renounce any aspect of the personality, including racial identification, in order to conform to the rest of society.

In approaching adulthood, the adolescent faces the task of establishing an identity as a man or woman. The succeeding task of personality development will be the challenge of finding intimacy and a relationship to the world of work and creativity, in which both competition and the opportunity for cooperation abound. In contemporary America, this coming into adulthood is not marked by the rituals of passage that some other cultures offer. This passage is a far more independent and individual one, and it tests the individual's mastery of the previous personality tasks. If the individual has not accepted who he is and what he represents, if he has not achieved a sense of peace and pride in his ethnic identity, the problems are compounded.

Grier and Cobbs, poignantly delineating some of the problems associated with ethnic identity for blacks. note that the blonde, blue-eyed, small-featured, white girl, the standard of American beauty, is a tragic model for the girl of minority heritage.[20] The black child has felt it and so has the Oriental, Hispanic, and Indian child. But nowhere is the issue of racial difference more emotionally enjoined than in the area of sex. The culture fears that the minority male's sexuality is exceeded only by its own expectations. The stereotypes of the black man as "stud," the Oriental as "knower of all mysteries," the Indian as "savage," and the Mexican as "permissive" are all associated with the myths and wishes of a prejudiced society.

The minority 15-year-old who fears girls as much as the white boy finds himself in a no-win predicament. He is unable to fulfill anyone's expectations. How does he feel about himself? How should he feel? What should he be like? Whom should he be like? What models should he use? Where do minority children look for their heroes? Whom do they emulate, wish to become? The process of identification is essential in the early school years to provide proper emotional growth, and yet in the absence of solid heroes and models, what is the minority child to do? Grier and Cobbs gave expression to the predicament:

[20] William H. Grier and Price M. Cobbs, *Black Rage* (New York: Bantam Books, 1968).

Black merchants were nonexistent; black politicians floated in a curious, nonexistence, far removed from the seats of power. The black men were left pretty much to the fields of entertainment and education as areas in which advancement was possible.[21]

Yet some changes have begun to occur. Bennett's *Before the May-flower* offers a documented and researched account of American history in which black persons come alive.[22] These are people who become heroes to children. There is, however, a danger with heroes. They can become one-dimensional and aloof from those things a child faces in himself—anxiety, conflict, uncertainty, and doubts of self-worth. There is a need, therefore, for objects for identification closer to home—people to associate with and to emulate. The experience of adults in facing their ethnicity, origins, and identity becomes, when shared with the child, an essential template for the development of that child's sense of worth.

In Madison, Wisconsin, McArdle and Young held classroom discussions on racial identity with a group of black and white high school students. Their report underlines the value of ethnic identity:

> As the sessions continued, the power of the cohesive black group appeared to frighten the whites. . . . The whites were learning that verbal acceptance was not enough. They unconsciously tried to strip the Negro of his identity and heritage by denying any differences in socioculture backgrounds. This, they thought, was one way of saying "We're all alike." The blacks were proud to point out the differences and especially to stress the importance of not "acting white." [23]

In 1969 this group was struggling with an issue that is not appreciated fully even in 1976—the value of being different. Healthy ethnic identity is defined as accepting one's own distinct characteristics and seeing them as valuable and worthwhile.

American society, in its overall process of understanding and accommodating ethnic identity, has come a long way toward overcoming the cultural stereotypes that even a short time ago plagued even those in scientific circles. The prevalence of the view that race and character were combined was tragic. As late as 1914, for example, the psychiatrist Lind spoke of the psychological activities of the "pure-blooded Negro"

---

[21] Ibid., p. 116.

[22] Lerone Bennett, *Before the Mayflower* (Baltimore: Penguin, 1966).

[23] Clare G. McArdle and Nancy F. Young, "Classroom Discussion of Racial Identity or How Can We Make It Without 'Acting White'?" *American Journal of Orthopsychiatry*, 40 (January 1970), p. 135.

in America as simplistic and childlike.[24] Szasz recently reviewed an 1851 report by Cartwright asserting that Negroes were biologically inferior to whites and that this necessitated their being kept and looked after as slaves. Cartwright provoked disagreement even in his own time, but the culture still expected only simplistic, inferior behavior and regarded anything else as deviant.[25]

This historical frame has to be a part of any detailed, thoughtful, and careful examination of the origins and effects of prejudice in particular individuals. Waite's description of the treatment of an adolescent black girl and the impact of that experience on clinical theory reflects a careful consideration of how an adolescent can be helped to establish an ethnic identity. This patient's problems included a difficulty in overcoming her feeling that, "I'm a Negro, therefore I'm bad." [26]

All minority children, and indeed all youth, are endangered by the possibility of identity diffusion. The issue of the individual in relation to the group becomes a major point of consideration. For some time emphasis was placed on brotherhood and similarity. The "melting pot" and its related concepts have unwittingly provoked identity diffusion in some youth. This has led to the development of a tension between identity as a unique individual and identity as derived from association with a large group, for example, an "American" identity. The problems experienced in the attempt to achieve identity are not unique to the minority child, although he may be considerably more vulnerable and suffer greater pain. All youths see themselves as isolated, doubt their own self-image, and are unsure about their appearances. They tend to perceive minor weaknesses in themselves, exaggerate their importance, and thereby suffer from identity diffusion. They feel alienated and, at times, even ashamed of their own families. For the minority child, this may take the form of a sense of shame about the family traditions, appearances, or role.

The challenge is to find a way for youth to come to terms with their background and heritage so that these contribute to a sense

[24] John E. Lind, "The Dream as a Simple Wish-Fulfillment in the Negro," *Psychoanalytic Review*, 1 (1914), p. 295.

[25] Thomas S. Szasz, "The Same Slave: An Historical Note on the Use of Medical Diagnosis as Justificatory Rhetoric," *American Journal of Psychotherapy*, 25 (April 1971), pp. 228–239.

[26] Richard R. Waite, "The Negro Patient and Clinical Theory," *Journal of Consulting and Clinical Psychology*, 32 (August 1968), p. 429.

of positive, solid, useful identity—an identity not diffused, but solidly introjected as "me." Youths whose identity diffusion has been intensified by their sense of being different are not limited to those ordinarily seen as belonging to a minority. They include not just the blacks or the Hispanics, but also those of Slavic origins as well as the Irish, women, and the physically handicapped. The degree of alienation that these children feel may not be as great as that felt by children of a more clearly identified racial minority. They may not feel the pressure of a minority identity as continually as children of more obvious minority characteristics, but the experiences are similar. At times, the poignancy and emotional pangs they feel of being different may be similar to those of other minority children.

IMPLICATIONS FOR SOCIAL POLICY

Society has not placed a premium on the identity of the child. The internal and immediately external environment of children has been an area largely ignored by the social planner. Yet much of what is known about individual identity formation can be translated into social policy and action. The area that demands greatest emphasis is early childhood. If social policy is to affect large numbers of children, it must be brought to bear in early childhood, as early perhaps as conception.

Planning for a broad program of early childhood services should include prenatal care and obstetrical care, visiting nurse services and homemaker services, day care, mental health services, and a cooperative package of social services for needy families. Planning for the development of a network of services utilizing many agencies and involving different dimensions of concern for the child and his identity must also be considered in translating the basic considerations of the child's psychological environment into a social program. Such an approach to social policy would need to include the following specific considerations:

1. Adequate prenatal care includes emotional support through education, expectant-mother groups, abortion counseling, and, whenever necessary, marital counseling. Part of these services can be counseling to help the pregnant woman to cope with her ethnic and racial identity.

2. Adequate birth control information needs to be available. The child needs parents who from the beginning can help him develop his own sense of worth and identity. The unprepared or unwilling parent cannot do this.

3. Parent preparation programs to educate parents to the emotional needs of the child; to inform them about his growth and development; and to foster an awareness of the importance of helping him establish a comfortable relationship in his own mind regarding his origins and identity. The same process can help the parent with his own feelings about his ethnic origins, so that he can transmit confidence and pride to his child.

4. Integrated education should begin early, perhaps at 18 months, to expose the child to children different from himself. The staff of a day care center should be taught how children develop a sense of self and a pride in their own ethnicity.

5. Early bilingual education should be available and should teach the child in the language of his own home while at the same time introducing him to the dominant language in the culture. The child cannot be placed in a situation where no one speaks his language if he is expected to lay down the initial building blocks of a solid sense of personal worth.

6. As the child reaches an age of racial awareness (4 or 5), he needs to be exposed to the values of difference. It is at this age—and continuing through junior high school—that television becomes perhaps the most effective, broad-reaching means of conveying these values.

7. In junior high or earlier there should be mandatory courses focusing on the child's understanding of emotions and of relationships. This will help prepare him for family life and for parenthood. It would include providing the youngster with information about child development. This can be related to education about the importance of individual identity, pride, and ethnic sense.

8. Throughout the school experience careful attention should be given to teaching materials to insure that adequate objects for identification and emulation from all ethnic, racial, and both sexual groups are available. Each child should have ample opportunity to identify with others like himself and to recognize similarities. This has not generally been the case for the minority child; but it is a matter that can be changed through social policy.

CONCLUSION

There remains the problem of the fusion of prejudice and aggression, which transcends a sense of ethnic identity. The experience of small children who have the early opportunity to experience themselves and others in a way that encourages the value and importance of difference may help reduce their potential for prejudice and aggression. However, many questions remain regarding the roots of prejudice. The development of identity is enormously complex, and its study technical. There is no doubt that the quest for an understanding of ethnicity will require decades of research and observation. The language of today may seem out of keeping with the understanding that will have been achieved twenty years from now. It is certain, however, that the basic concepts available now will be part of the foundation on which the future understanding is built. Perhaps society, applying what is known about ethnic identity, will provide for a more effective pluralism—a pluralism that will foster the value of individualism and personal identity—and thus create a society that will value the identity of the child as one of its most important resources.

Environmental Influences on Social Functioning: The Black Experience

LEON CHESTANG

Leon Chestang, MSW, is Assistant Professor, School of Social Service Administration, University of Chicago, Chicago, Illinois.

EDITORS' COMMENT

Chestang focuses on the dilemma of living in two worlds and the duality that develops within the personality structure of an individual when his membership in a certain group prohibits the fusion of his own unique identity with the larger world around him. When society admits an individual to full participation in its culture, his immediate world (which Chestang calls the nutritive world of family, friends, and community) merges with his larger world (called the sustentative world of employment, education, and status). Partial or circumscribed participation in the culture poses a dilemma for the individual between the competing demands of his psychological identity and his survival in the larger culture.

Chestang explores the dynamics of human behavior under such circumstances. Although the subjects of his study are blacks, the concepts may be applied to any ethnic group having to negotiate a hostile environment. The explicit social policy implications pertain especially to the provision of social treatment, but recognition of this duality has implications for many areas of social policy, especially education. Norton also touches on the theme of duality in personality structure, and her application of it is to housing policy.

A major gap in social work knowledge relates to the role of environment as an influence on social functioning. Although significant theoretical advances have been made in understanding the development of personality and its interaction with the environment, these theories have concentrated on illuminating the effect of environment on psychic structure as it was described by Freud. The result of this focus has been to heighten the awareness of the individual's response to the environment but at the same time to divert attention from the environment itself. Thus, knowledge of the individual as a reactor to the environment surpasses comprehension of the environment itself, particularly the role of the macroenvironment as actor in shaping and molding the individual. More specifically, there are no concepts adequate to the task of explaining the interrelationship between microenvironmental factors, such as family and a macroenvironmental force like social structure; nor are there acceptable explanations of the effect of these micro- and macroenvironmental forces as they influence social functioning.

The objective of this essay, therefore, is to explore the influence of environmental factors—both large and small—on social functioning. This will be done by examining the social conditions confronting black people in American society and relating them to the adaptations they have produced. A framework for a more accurate and comprehensive understanding of the interplay between micro- and macroenvironmental forces and their effect on social functioning will be set forth. In deriving the formulations and in constructing the framework presented here, the author has relied most heavily on interpretations growing out of his own analysis. At the same time, some of the concepts embodied in these formulations reflect existing psychosocial and sociocultural theory. The attempt, therefore, will be to show the connections between the author's propositions and those set forth in relevant existing theory.

The term "black experience," which has become part of the American vocabulary, serves as a multipurpose phrase that encompasses events and processes but that creates difficulties in communication and analysis. It connotes the deferred dreams and frustrated aspirations of a people oppressed by society. It expresses what Bennett, in celebrating the triumph of a man over a social order that would degrade him, has called "a certain dark joy." [1] It may also convey the ideas of a culture, style, and social pattern developed to cope with the life situation to which society consigns the black man.

These varied connotations reflect isolated aspects of the black experience; but they fail to synthesize and specify the process of this encounter between person and environment. Without such synthesis and specificity, it is impossible to communicate the notion with sufficient conceptual substance and clarity to make it operationally useful. The concept of the black experience finds its origin in the minority status of black people and the prevailing social attitudes toward them. These attitudes—negative and pervasive—have potent implications for the character development of the black individual.[2]

INJUSTICE, INCONSISTENCY, IMPOTENCE

Three conditions, socially determined and institutionally supported, characterize the black experience: social injustice, societal inconsistency, and personal impotence. The failure of many majority-group Americans to appreciate the psychic impact of these conditions can be attributed to the absence of what Warren calls an "institutional thought structure" supporting any but an individual-deficit model for understanding social problems.[3] Moreover, the failure to perceive

[1] Lerone Bennett, *The Negro Mood* (Chicago: Johnson Publishing Co., 1964), pp. 61–73.

[2] *See* Kenneth Clark, *Dark Ghetto* (New York: Harper & Row, 1965), p. xxiii, for a discussion of the uniqueness of the black experience; and Leon Chestang, *Character Development in a Hostile Environment*, Occasional Paper, Number 3 (Chicago: School of Social Service Administration, University of Chicago, 1972).

[3] Roland L. Warren, "The Sociology of Knowledge and the Problems of the Inner Cities" (Waltham, Mass.: Brandeis University, 1970). (Mimeographed.)

the distinction between the nature of injustice and that of inconsistency, the ambiguity surrounding the role of each of the three elements in shaping the character of black persons, and the absence of substantive concepts related to the three elements add to the problem of articulating the black experience. There is a need for a view that incorporates environmental effects.

Social injustice is the denial of legal rights. Since laws represent group consensus, injustice is a violation of social agreements. When one group acts against another, the consequences reach the individual through the intermediary of his group, rendering the effects diffuse rather than direct. Social injustice, then, is a group phenomenon resulting in violence to the character development of members of groups that are treated differently.

Social inconsistency is the institutionalized disparity between word and deed. It is social immorality perpetrated on the oppressed group by the manners, morals, and traditions of the majority group. In a person-to-person transaction, it is the individual expression of group rejection, a personalized injustice that attacks the individual without his group supports and that the individual takes personally. Each act of this institutionalized behavior deprives the black person of the feelings of self-worth and esteem he has derived from his attempts to achieve acceptance through adhering to the values, norms, and beliefs prescribed by society. Since it expresses the informal and unofficial rejection of blacks, societal inconsistency leaves the individual without recourse to regulatory agencies and courts of law. There is no official code saying that black skin is unattractive, black art unaesthetic, black culture uncivilized, or black persons unworthy of respect. These are expressions of manners, morals, and traditions whose correction is beyond the power of the courts.

No discussion of the black experience, however abbreviated, can avoid reference to the impotence felt by blacks as they try to effect changes in their lives. The pervasiveness of this feeling has been recounted by numerous writers of both races for many years.[4] Impotence, a result of social inconsistency and injustice, is the sense of powerlessness to influence the environment. On an individual level, it is the feeling of the father unable to secure employment and there-

---

[4] *See,* for example, Alexis de Tocqueville, *Democracy in America,* Vol. 1 (New York: Vantage Books, 1954); Clark, op. cit.; Eldridge Cleaver, *Soul on Ice* (New York: Delta Books, 1968); E. Franklin Frazier, *Black Bourgeoisie* (New York: Collier Books, 1962); and Gunnar Myrdal, *An American Dilemma* (New York: Harper & Bros., 1944).

fore unable to support his family. It is the experience of the black man consigned to prison because he is unable to secure justice from the courts. And impotence is the social role enacted by the black politician who recites platitudes issued from "the man," just as it was the role of his father who bowed, grinned, and scraped.

This impotence is furthered by social institutions. A recent study conducted by the Chicago Urban League found that blacks, who account for 40 percent of that city's total population, hold less than 3 percent of the decision-making positions in the city's major institutions, including business, social welfare, and education.[5] Similar testimony to the impotence of blacks can be found in every city, town, and village in the nation.

BLACK CULTURE AND CHARACTER DEVELOPMENT

The peculiar social structure confronting blacks offers an excellent focus for exploration. This is true for the reasons stated at the beginning of this essay and also because such a focus affords an opportunity to demonstrate the thesis that blacks reside in two cultures at once. The three crucial elements of the black experience have been identified as social injustice, societal inconsistency, and personal impotence.[6] These conditions, together with the development of competence in a behavioral style designed to combat their negative consequences, represent the progenitors of black character. The essential feature of this style is a duality of response stemming from the experience of functioning in two cultures.[7] Any explanation of the origins of black character is, in fact, incomplete until this crucial circumstance—functioning in two cultures—is added. What follows is an attempt to study the nature of this duality and its psychosocial dynamics as a force in black character development. The thesis is that the uniqueness of the black experience resides in the imperative that members of this group live in two cultures and that effective social functioning under such conditions requires the development of a dual response.

Two points of clarification regarding this focus are necessary. The first involves culture and its powerful influence on individual behavior, an influence too often neglected or treated superficially by social workers, psychologists, and psychiatrists. Benedict has shown the

[5] "Negroes in Policy-Making Positions in Chicago: A Study in Black Powerlessness" (Chicago: Chicago Urban League, 1968), p. 5. (Mimeographed.)

[6] Chestang, op. cit.

[7] Ibid.

importance of relating the individual's responses to the behaviors validated by his culture.[8] Suppose, however, that an individual dwells in two cultures. And suppose, as in the case of American society, that black persons possess both the culture of the dominant group and their own.

Benedict's observation is especially pertinent to this examination of the behavior of black individuals who live in two cultures and whose "congenial responses," as Benedict termed responses compatible with the person's principles, are heavily determined by this fact. But what if the congenial responses singled out in one culture conflict with those singled out in the other? What if the cultural demands of participation in one conflict with the reality of participation in the other? Further, what if the psychological and social value of one is thought to be less than that of the other? And what if the carriers of these two cultures make such assessments themselves? Also, what is the psychological price exacted from individuals living in such a condition? These questions provide a framework for this study, and they highlight the significance of culture as a focal point in the explorations into black character development.

The second point of clarification involves character development as distinct from personality development. In studying the response of a group to the social conditions under which its members live, individual character structure—the ways of thinking, feeling, and acting—must be considered. This article is not concerned with the variations and peculiarities indicating the differences between and among individuals. These are many and rich in their diversity; but it is this very diversity between and among individuals that tends to veil those elements of character shared by all members of the group and that are paramount in our effort to delineate those traits which they share in common. The primary interest here is in what Fromm has called "social character":

> The social character comprises only a selection of traits, the essential nucleus of the character structure of most members of a group which has developed as a result of the basic experiences and mode of life common to that group.[9]

Understanding one individual most fully is best achieved through an examination of the differentiating elements between him and

[8] Ruth Benedict, *Patterns of Culture* (Boston: Houghton Mifflin Co., 1934), p. 254.

[9] Erich Fromm, *Escape From Freedom* (New York: Holt, Rinehart & Winston, 1941), pp. 304–305.

others, but, as Fromm says, "If we want to understand how human energy is channeled and operates as a productive force in a given social order, then the social character deserves our main interest."[10]

SOCIAL CONDITIONS FOSTERING CULTURAL DUALITY

The concept of marginality provides an inadequate description of the relations between the black person and the larger society. Marginality implies an existence on the fringes of two societies but full membership in neither. The peculiar nature of American society and the peculiar circumstances of blacks in that society cause them to develop a cultural duality. A review of the societal factors and social circumstances creating this duality in their cultural adaptation illuminates this point.

The national credo of the melting pot has been a guiding force in shaping national policies and the national character. Freedom, justice, and equality are the guiding principles determining the sociopolitical stance and self-image of the American citizen. When black Americans are denied these rights, the larger society frequently resorts to rationalizations about the blacks' unreadiness or about racial inferiority, or it may dawdle in the time-worn debate about social change through revolution versus evolution. These responses preserve the cultural heritage of democratic pluralism by excusing the exceptions, and they protect the majority's self-image by denying personal culpability. Although such maneuvers lessen the discomfort felt by members of the dominant society, they also create a social and emotional split in the acculturative process for the black person seeking to enter the mainstream of American life.

His African heritage largely erased through slavery, the American black, through interaction with the dominant culture, adopted the prevailing legal ethical philosophy of the melting pot. He believed in its implications of equality, justice, and freedom. When the society's institutions, customs, and codes constrained the black man from realizing these rights for himself, they became symbols rather than realities for him. Thus, the black person incorporated these principles as psychological abstractions rather than operational realities. He became, as it were, a bearer *of* the culture whose participation *in* the culture was circumscribed and conditional. This dilemma imposes a special adaptive task for blacks in the acculturative process.

Similarly, although blacks have been relegated to a caste position

10 Fromm, op. cit., p. 305.

in American society, the caste system has had a certain flexibility. Over the years, blacks in general have interacted with varying degrees of intimacy with the larger society, and a few blacks in particular have had more intense contact with the society. In their roles as household servants, professionals, leaders of the black community, and ever-present citizens of a second order, blacks have learned and internalized the essence of the dominant culture.

Further, because the controls of the economic resources are lodged in the larger society, blacks are dependent on it for their very survival. Obviously, this situation required interaction with the culture at large, but, more important, it defined and prescribed the occupational choice of black Americans and their psychological inclination toward such choices as well. This latter point is crucial. Even with limited choices, the black pursued his vocation with the goal of acquiring the accoutrements that come with membership in the society at large. If, because of the nature of society, he did not succeed on a practical level, he succeeded on a psychological level. Frazier asserted that

> the black bourgeoisie live largely in a world of make-believe, [and] the masks they wear to play their sorry roles conceal the feelings of inferiority and of insecurity and the frustrations that haunt their inner lives.[11]

But if this is true, these bourgeois can perhaps be allowed this fault, for it was acquired under the burden of carrying a culture in their minds that they could not exercise in their lives.

Similarly, the styles and psychological inclinations of the black poor, in many instances, reflect this duality of culture. Their emphasis on "makin' it" and "gettin' over" cannot be adequately explained in terms of the ethos of personal and social deprivation. The explanation for this behavior and the psychological inclinations that precede it resides in the molding force of culture:

> The vast proportion of all individuals who are born into any society always, and whatever the idiosyncracies of its institutions, assume . . . the behavior dictated by that society. . . . It does not matter whether, with the Northwest Coast Indians, it requires delusions of self-reference, or with our own civilization the amassing of possessions.[12]

The black poor, like their brothers of greater means, are born into society with a common badge of exclusion from its culture. But

---

[11] E. Franklin Frazier, *Black Bourgeoisie* (New York: Collier Books, 1962), p. 176.

[12] Benedict, op. cit., p. 254.

that culture towers like a mountain above a valley and casts its shadow on all who dwell below, coaxing them to ascend to its pinnacle. The apparent exaggerations and pretentiousness in poor blacks' pursuit of this goal represent their efforts to live out a cultural ideal from which they are excluded, and it reflects their adaptation to an impossible situation. Their behavioral manifestation is a symbolic assertion of their humanity and, hence, of their acceptability and competence to participate in the only culture they know. When the larger society refused to acknowledge their participation in the culture, in essence it denied validity to their being. Thus thwarted, they have developed a character split that distorts their responses as carriers of the culture. If their behavior is caricatured and overstated, it is because their very existence embodies the contradiction of being (in the culture) and not being (in it) at the same time. Therefore, what we refer to as "black culture" is in reality the manifestation of the mediation and synthesis of two cultures, the one obligatory and learned by exposure, and the other developed out of necessity.

This is not to say that black culture is simply a vulgarization of the dominant culture. Its expression represents a creative adaptation to a set of sociopolitical circumstances that defines the black condition. It is the subjective experience of this condition that gives rise to the black experience. Flowing from that experience is a set of social arrangements, a code of beliefs and values, a pattern of institutional forms, and a host of human creations designed to regulate interpersonal relations and to express their subjective reality. This constellation of responses, of course, represents black culture.

There is yet another peculiar circumstance that the black person must confront: He is psychologically tied to the larger society through incorporation of its values, norms, and beliefs and through the unique nature of his arrival and existence in the United States. The psychological bond with the larger society can be explained principally by acculturation and history. How the eradication of his own culture obliged him to adopt the prevailing culture without full participation in it has already been discussed. It is necessary to reemphasize, however, that culture consists not only of objective phenomena; it is equally and more profoundly subjective experience. Moreover, the objective phenomena of culture cannot be discussed apart from the subjective experience of it. Hence, for the black person, the incorporation of the dominant culture means that the culture became a part of his being, albeit a dormant part. Nevertheless, he could not reject the dominant culture—nor can we discount its influence on him

—for he has been shaped as much by the prevailing social system as by the system that developed out of his exclusion from it.

Thus, in spite of their condition in American society, blacks do not, as a group, feel alien to their country. Their identification with their country of origin parallels, at maximum, that of most other groups who adopted the New World. And their problems with their relationship to the larger society are comparable to those of the Europeans who came after them: how to be true to ethnic identity and the new culture at the same time. With few exceptions, the black individual, like the white ethnic, has yielded to the molding force of culture and has chosen the path of assimilation.

The conclusion that remnants of the blacks' African heritage should be more persistent and tenacious than those of, say, the Irish or the Poles is both surprising and erroneous. Consider the census of 1860, which reported that one-fourth of all the slaves in the United States were held in parcels of fifteen to twenty slaves. Herskovits comments on this phenomenon:

> This means that about one-half of the slaves had a distinct facilitation in obtaining an appreciable share in the social heritage of their masters. . . . *The very fact that Negroes were slaves linked them as a whole more closely to the whites than any scheme of wage-labor could well have done.*[13] [Italics added.]

This close link to white society and culture has persisted over the years, and in many ways, the passage of time and the relaxation of some of the more blatant racial barriers have strengthened it. Blacks, therefore, feel dispossessed rather than alienated. In contrast to the modern immigrant, they feel not like strangers in a foreign land, but like rejected members of a family.

What parades as absolute contempt for white American culture is a response to blacks' entanglement in the paradoxical state of possession without participation in the dominant culture and masks a strong ambivalence toward it. The frequently cited love-hate syndrome can be explained by this paradox and offers testimony to the existence of a psychological bond. Consider the cyclical popularity of ideas about separation as an adaptation to the inequities of society. Such ideas originate and recur in proportion to the degree of frustration felt by blacks at given points in time. All the foregoing facts speak less to a self-depreciating pursuit of unrequited love than to a pilgrimage to achieve a group birthright.

[13] Melville J. Herskovits, *The Myth of the Negro Past* (Boston: Beacon Press, 1958), p. 120.

Up to this point the side of the paradox that illustrates the black person's orientation to and possession of the dominant culture has been stressed. Now those conditions and forces germinal to the evolution of an alternative cultural pattern among blacks must be considered. Along with them it is necessary to develop further the conceptualization of how this evolution occurs and how it affects social work practice.

NURTURING AND SUSTAINING ENVIRONMENTS

In an effort to understand the nature of the duality in the black experience and culture, it is necessary to turn again to the concept of culture. Because it encompasses all human creations—tools, institutions, customs, beliefs, and so on—culture can be regarded as the sum total of man's external environment and his psychological predisposition toward that environment. Understanding the experience of the black person requires an examination of his functioning and his psychological predispositions and set toward two environments.

For purposes of clarity and focus, it is helpful to distinguish between what may be called the sustentative aspects of culture—tools, weapons, shelter, material goods, and services—and the nutritive aspects—attitudes and beliefs, ideas and judgments, codes, institutions, arts and sciences, philosophy and social organization. The sustentative aspects of culture are objective cultural expressions, but offering livelihood, physical comfort, and safety. In essence, the sustentative aspects of culture are those that respond to man's basic instinct, survival. The nutritive aspects, on the other hand, are the expressive features of culture embodying and influencing thinking, feeling, and behavior—in other words, the social character of a people. It is through these facets of culture that the individual experiences psychological and social gratification, derives an identity, feels intimacy, and finds a haven from the assaults of the larger society.

When the society admits an individual to full participation in its culture, the sustentative and nutritive aspects are merged. The symbols and objects manifesting the culture evoke in him feelings of loyalty, pride, and identification. Implied in such a state of affairs is a unified wholeness between the objective creations and the subjective experience of them. Hence the American flag or the Empire State Building are American not only because Americans designed and constructed them, but because they are invested with beliefs, attitudes, and emotions related to this country's history and ideals, which, as it were, live in these constructions rendering them no longer simply things but monuments.

But what if the individual is divorced from society or is allowed only partial and circumscribed participation in it? Under such circumstances, what form does the individual's participation in the culture take? Such exclusion results in two alternatives for the individual. He can succumb to the erosive denials of his humanity, or he can, as Merton has indicated, perform adaptive maneuvers to preserve his integrity.[14] In the case of the black person interacting with the wider society, to choose the first alternative is to elect an empty physical survival while surrendering the dignity that is the essence of humanity. To choose the second, when one considers the cost, whether in the output of psychological energy or in the threat, under some circumstances, to physical survival, indicates the power of the impulse toward being—the inner push toward self-realization.

Whether a person chooses one or the other of these alternatives is determined by the strength of the two forces that govern the direction of his course of action. These two interacting forces, being and survival, are intrinsic to man, and the quality of his character rests on the extent to which they are in harmony. The importance of these notions to the thesis of this essay is crucial, and they are not pursued still further here only for lack of space. Enough has been said, however, so that the ideas presented above can be considered in the context of their implications for the social functioning of black persons in the black community.

As has already been pointed out, the social conditions confronting blacks—social injustice, societal inconsistency, and personal impotence —cause a split in the acculturative process resulting in the development of a duality of culture. This duality is composed of the sustaining environment and nurturing environment. In this essay attention is focused only on the latter, but it will help to outline the former.

The sustaining environment consists of the survival needs of man: goods and services, political power, economic resources. It is largely through this environment that status is conferred and power exercised. It is the world of the larger society. The black individual is propelled toward it by the need for survival, and, because he is denied full participation in it, he makes an instrumental adaptation to it.

The nurturing environment, the black community, differs from the sustaining environment in two ways: First, it affords the individual emotional support, cultural values, family relationships, and sup-

[14] Robert K. Merton, *Social Theory and Social Structure* (rev. ed.; Glencoe, Ill.: Free Press, 1957), pp. 187–188.

portive institutions. His relationship to this world is expressive. This is to say that within this environment, the individual experiences a sense of wholeness and identification. And second, the black individual is pulled toward this world by the force that has here been called "being." This latter term suggests that the pull is toward self-realization and dignity.

Once it is recognized that the duality of culture that characterizes the black experience has a decided impact on character development, it becomes possible to see more clearly that the depreciated character (the incorporation by blacks of the wider society's negative attributions) is an adaptation to the sustaining environment and that the transcendent character (the incorporation of positive images from the black community) emerges and is supported by the nurturing environment. But because the nurturing and sustaining environments, to use Parsons's term, interpenetrate, both influence and condition the emergence of the transcendent character.[15] It is beyond the scope of this essay to discuss in detail the influence of the sustaining environment, but it can be noted that it is likely the push of survival—the force which prompts the black person's adaptation to the sustaining environment—that gives impetus to the development of the transcendent character.

The aim here, however, is to relate the understanding of cultural duality among black persons to particular cultural patterns expressed within the nurturing environment—family patterns, behavioral styles, and child-rearing patterns, for example—and to place these in a theoretical context that enhances the understanding of their purpose and function. It has been argued by Ladner and Herskovits that much of black culture consists of African survivals.[16] These remnants should not be misconstrued, however, as the essence of black culture. Although significant holdovers might be expected among immigrants who interact benignly with new societies under conditions of cultural pluralism, they can hardly be expected to exist among blacks, whose condition in American society is fraught with cultural depreciation and personal depreciation. All that has been learned from cultural anthropology suggests that when two groups come together and when one of them is in a minority status, the minority group seeks assimilation or at least accommodation in the dominant society. When the minority group's culture has been eliminated, the thrust is all the

[15] Talcott Parsons and Robert F. Bales, *Family, Socialization and Interaction Process* (Glencoe, Ill.: Free Press, 1955), p. 32.

[16] Herskovits, op. cit., pp. 292–299; and Joyce A. Ladner, *Tomorrow's Tomorrow* (Garden City, N.Y.: Doubleday & Co., 1972).

more decidedly in the direction of assimilation. Therefore, myths about Africanisms and cultural survivals do not completely explain black cultural patterns.

A more reasonable and complete explanation is that, although black culture reflects a stylistic resemblance to its African origin, its more profound elements developed in adaptation to the social circumstances in America. Thus, the important role of religion among blacks. This institution serves the psychological purpose of strengthening the individual in the face of his impotence against the social structure and the sociopolitical function of providing an outlet for his talents and abilities, as well as furnishing a focal point for community organization.

Ladner's study of the black woman has amply demonstrated that the roles she assumes in caring for her family even when the male is absent and her strength of character, often approaching mythological proportions, are in large measure adaptations to the necessities imposed by the social structure.[17] If strict child-rearing patterns and early assumption of responsibility by children, especially among the lower class, are frequently observed phenomena, these patterns testify more to the exigencies of survival within a particular social structure than to any innate propensities of a people. Similar explanations could be offered for other black cultural characteristics. It is enough to say, however, that within the nurturing environment, the values, norms, and traditions as well as the cultural patterns and behavioral styles are designed to nurture the individual, to maintain his dignity, and to promote the development of the transcendent character.

Certain observers may find the cultural patterns, behaviors, attitudes, and responses peculiar. It should be recalled, however, that these responses were developed as adaptations to the hostility of the sustaining environment. Theoreticians of both the psychosocial and the sociocultural schools have found that responses such as those described here result from conditions similar to those faced by black persons. Erikson and Merton spoke pointedly on the effects of social structure on the individual's behavior.[18] It can be seen, therefore, that a variety of patterns develop as a result of this split in culture and that these patterns will be reflected both in the quality of the relationship with the sustaining environment and in the form taken by the responses to the nurturing environment. This finding is,

[17] Ladner, op. cit., pp. 44–46.

[18] Erik Erikson, *Childhood and Society* (New York: W. W. Norton & Co., 1963), p. 230; and Merton, op. cit., pp. 193–211.

of course, not new. The value of this effort lies in its attempt to articulate systematically the process by which adaptation to particular social conditions occurs.

IMPLICATIONS FOR SOCIAL WELFARE POLICY

Social work's contribution lies, as noted earlier, in its effort to articulate the nature of the black experience and the process by which the resultant duality of black culture occurs. These matters have implications for social welfare policy and especially for program administration, personnel recruitment, and staff development. Some steps can be suggested that seem compatible with the circumstances of personality development outlined in this article.

Since black culture arises from the efforts of black people to master a peculiar set of social circumstances, social welfare programs should respect the validity of the coping mechanisms displayed by the group and the integrity of individuals whose life-styles vary from the American norm. This implies that social welfare organizations should operate from policies that recognize the social realities and constraints hampering members of this group in obtaining employment, housing, and other public services. The requirement of employment as a condition for receiving public assistance, for example, should be flexible so that the reality of discrimination would be considered in the implementation of such a policy. Because blacks may be confronted with discriminatory practices in obtaining needed services, social welfare organizations should establish, as a matter of course, the practices of advocacy either through negotiation or through the courts to protect their clients. The necessity of using the courts holds true for both public and private social welfare organizations.

Since 1965 wide attention has been given to bringing personnel recruitment and staffing in social welfare organizations to reflect the client populations, and a number of encouraging developments are in progress. Outstanding among these is the increase in the number of blacks employed in such programs. Insofar as these developments reflect an awareness of their symbolic and practical meaning to black clientele they may be interpreted, in terms of this analysis, as positive change. Unfortunately, many organizations perceive only the symbolic meaning of employing blacks, and tokenism is the result. What is called for is an open system that recognizes the negative effects on black persons when they are denied employment in spite of competence.

Although the employment of blacks has positive symbolic and

practical implications, the analysis presented in this article does not support the argument that service to blacks is effective only when provided by members of their own group. Such an argument ignores the evidence that it is the social conditions under which blacks live that largely accounts for their problems in obtaining and utilizing services. Thus, changing the race of staff without changing unjust and inconsistent institutional practices is fruitless.

Guiding staff development and training programs must be an increased awareness of and sensitivity to the duality in black culture. Staff charged with serving the black community must recognize that members of this group share many of the same aspirations and motivations held by members of the wider society. What is different is more likely to be the avenues open to blacks for achieving their goals, their styles in approaching them, and the cultural forms whereby they express their desire to actualize themselves. Indeed, even there patterns may be hard to discern among many blacks. For this reason, it is more important to emphasize here the need for staff to respond to blacks as individuals who will differ from one another in the same manner as members of other groups. Some commonalities related to their status in society, however, will be apparent. The notion that blacks may make an instrumental relationship with what is called the sustaining environment is noteworthy.

This proposition suggests that some blacks will relate pragmatically to social welfare organizations but view the benefits and services from a perspective different from that of other clients. This is an important consideration, for at the root of much of the staff frustration and program ineffectiveness associated with serving the black community are the different goals that blacks attach to programs compared to those seen by program developers. Thus, someone might participate in counseling services, not because of the service's potential for enhancing personal growth, but because financial benefits are contingent on receiving the counseling. Training programs, particularly those with little relevance to available or desirable jobs, are endured rather than made the object of hope and expended energy. Similarly, service on advisory boards, especially when the decision-making prerogative is limited or retained elsewhere, may become a platform for self-aggrandizement. These reactions on the part of black clients are to be understood as natural responses to their social conditions and status. If these essentially unproductive responses are to be reduced, social welfare policies and programs, including the training of staff, must function in ways that offer clients a realistic opportunity to achieve the goals for which such policies were established.

Residential Environment and Black Self-Image

DOLORES NORTON

Dolores Norton, Ph.D., is Associate Professor, Graduate School of Social Work and Social Research, Bryn Mawr College, Bryn Mawr, Pennsylvania.

Editors' Comment

Norton's study, like Chestang's, focuses on the ways in which environment influences the personality and behavior of the individual, but it does so with the goal of exploring the implications for housing policy in a pluralistic society. Also like Chestang, Norton examines the duality of experience for the ethnic minority person. Using Mead and Erikson, Norton traces the development of the black self-image and relates it to the social and physical factors in the residential environment.

The relationship between current housing practices and personality structure is discussed. Norton balances personality factors against the tenacity of segregated housing that was demonstrated in Kantrowitz's study of New York segregation. Despite changes in income and open-housing laws, Norton advocates housing policies that will insure comprehensive residential services to all neighborhoods. The goals of such policies are to maximize the positive effect on as many ethnic or minority groups as possible and to develop human potential. Socioeconomic variables have long been recognized as important in formulating housing policy, and it is equally imperative that ethnic differences be recognized as well.

A concept of policy development that takes personality into account inevitably begins to explore the effects of the larger society and its social policies on the personality structure of individuals and groups. Consequently, this essay uses personality theory and social theory in tandem to help determine what kind of social policies and programs might best serve certain groups. Implicit throughout is the assumption that the United States is a pluralistic society composed of many different needs and experiences. A second assumption is that social policies whose positive effects reach as many groups as possible will be best for the total society. Of principal concern in this article are the preliminary findings of a study conducted in 1972 of black residential patterns in the Philadelphia metropolitan area.[1] The study is used in this article to draw out the implications for housing policy of the relationship between environment and black self-image.

RESIDENTIAL RACIAL PATTERNS

In 1970, 86 percent of the black population in forty-seven large cities was living in census tracts that were 50 percent or more black.[2]

[1] The study of black suburbanization patterns, which was titled "Black Residential Perceptions in the Philadelphia Metropolitan Area," was undertaken with the support of National Science Foundation, Research Applied to National Needs, Grants NSF–GI–29939 and GI–39220, and was conducted at the Fels Center of Government, University of Pennsylvania, and University City Science Center, Philadelphia, Pennsylvania. *See also* Phoebe H. Cottingham, "Black Income and Metropolitan Residential Dispersion," *Urban Affairs Quarterly,* 10 (March 1975), pp. 273–296.

[2] Elfriede F. Hoeber, "Separation and Dispersion of Blacks in Major Metropolitan Areas," unpublished manuscript (Washington, D.C.: Office of Economic Opportunity, Department of Housing and Urban Development, 1972).

Wherever there was black movement to the suburbs the same pattern of racial separation appeared to be maintained with black populations tending to cluster. The general explanation for this suburban pattern is that any movement by blacks to the suburbs is restricted and shaped by the low income of the black population and by racial discrimination. To relieve this situation, major governmental housing policies push for open housing legislation and stress the elimination of discriminatory housing practices by realtors and lending agencies.

However, preliminary findings of the Philadelphia study indicated that neither the passage of equal opportunity housing legislation nor the achievement of income parity appeared to have much effect on black suburbanization. Blacks simply do not appear inclined to move to the suburbs in any substantial numbers regardless of family income. For example, in the Philadelphia metropolitan area, the 1972 study showed that 5 percent of the blacks earning over $25,000 had moved to the suburbs compared to 27 percent of the whites earning the same income.[3]

Some studies have tentatively concluded that more than racial discrimination is involved, that blacks do not move to suburban white neighborhoods because they are strongly attached to black community institutions and social relations. Other observers have suggested that the residential preferences of blacks have been affected by recent changes in black attitudes toward integration.[4] Aberbach and Walker suggest that the increased support for black identity is accompanied by decreased black support for various forms of integration.[5] The preliminary findings of the study of black suburbanization in the Philadelphia area suggest that, although racial discrimination is a major factor in explaining black residential concentration, it may not be the total explanation. Whites may not be the only group that helps to maintain the segregated pattern.

According to the Philadelphia study, blacks negatively evaluate the experiences they assume black people undergo in a predominantly

[3] Cottingham, op. cit., p. 1.

[4] *See* "Federal Government's Role in the Achievement of Equal Opportunity in Housing," Hearing before the Civil Rights Oversight Committee of the Committee on Judiciary, House of Representatives, 92nd Congress, October 27, 1971 (Washington, D.C.: U.S. Government Printing Office, 1972); and *Equal Opportunity in Housing in the Delaware Valley Region* (Philadelphia, Pa.: Delaware Valley Regional Planning Commission, 1972).

[5] Joel D. Aberbach and Jack L. Walker, *Race in the City* (Boston: Little, Brown & Co., 1972), pp. 65–67.

white neighborhood. This may mean that blacks either consciously or unconsciously assume that a positive self-image for them and their children cannot be maintained in a white residential environment.

DEFINITION OF BLACK SELF-IMAGE

An individual's physical and social environment is most heavily influenced by the family in which he grows up. In the United States, a family's physical and social environment is most heavily influenced by its race and socioeconomic status; religious and ethnic factors are secondary. Race and class determine to a great extent where and how the family actually lives and who its friends are. All these variables in turn contribute to the experiences of the individual that lead to the development of self.

The term "self" refers to that conglomerate of consciousness, personality, attitudes, emotions, and perceptions that makes up the individual's identity and influences his behavior.[6] It is the sense of being that makes the individual an entity to himself. Adler describes the self as a unique configuration of motives, traits, interests, and values that intervene between the action of stimuli on the individual and the interpretation and reaction to those stimuli.[7]

The self emerges from the interaction between the heredity and the life experiences of the individual. The experiences of the individual are primarily determined by his physical environment (the concrete physical factors or conditions surrounding him) and his social environment (the mode and type of interaction with his own family and other significant people with whom he comes into contact).

No individual is shaped solely by relations with his physical and social environment. One's own unique heredity is also vital.[8] Although the same experience can affect different people in different ways, it is possible to generalize about the black self-image by considering the historical black experience.

Three common and powerful aspects of the black experience have

[6] Erik Erikson, *Identity, Youth and Crisis* (New York: W. W. Norton & Co., 1968).

[7] Alfred Adler, *Individual Psychology of Alfred Adler: A Systematic Presentation in Selections from His Writings*, Heinz L. Ansbacker and Rowena R. Ansbacker, eds. (New York: Basic Books, 1956), p. 177.

[8] George H. Mead, *Mind, Self and Society* (Chicago: University of Chicago Press, 1934), pp. 227–8.

led to similarities in personality among black people despite the variances in individual heredity:

1. Blacks came to this country as slaves and as such were considered property. Their only value was an economic one. In a Judeo-Christian culture, it was not possible to treat another human being as property without producing an ethical conflict. This conflict between the slave owners' actions and their religious beliefs was resolved by assigning a subhuman status to the slaves.

2. The slaves' color was different from that of the majority of the population and gave them high visibility. Slavery became synonymous with black, and since slaves were inferior, inferiority became synonymous with blacks.

3. These beliefs and attitudes led to the systematic, that is, not random but planned, physical and social exclusion of blacks from all the social, political, economic, and educational institutions of the society. These three factors eliminated virtually all opportunity for blacks to assimilate into the mainstream of American society. Blacks were forced to live in a physical, psychological, social, and economic world that was different from the white world. Historically, no black has been able to escape entirely the effects of this racism, regardless of where he went or how high a status he attained.

This common experience, born of pervasive prejudice and exclusion, is the basis for a certain type of orientation toward the larger white world. In an environment that has historically been hostile, it was inevitable that part of the black reaction to people and events would be individual and that at times some element of the reaction would be specifically black, similar to the reaction of most blacks. It is this common reaction resulting from pervasive prejudice and exclusion that is central to this discussion. Other ethnic and minority groups may exhibit similar kinds of double reactions in equally hostile situations.

DEVELOPMENT OF SELF

Although the complicated dynamics of the development of the personality cannot be described within the scope of this article, some common understanding of how the self develops is a necessary preliminary. Most personality and social theorists suppose that the self is social in essence and that it develops in a complex of interactions between the genetically given and the life or social experiences through which the individual learns his reality and becomes a self. This concept closely resembles the theories of personality development described by Adler, Mead, and Erikson.

In Mead's sociological concept of self, the peculiar character of the human social environment is primary. Mead stresses the development of the self as the result of the interaction between the unique "I," the individual, and the "me" or the reflection for the larger society, which he calls the "generalized other." [9] Similarly Erikson's concept of identity is defined as a "subjective sense of an invigorating sameness and continuity" which comes about as a fusion of personal and cultural factors.[10] Identity thus consists of an awareness of the style of one's individuality and of the "fact that this style coincides with the sameness and continuity of one's meaning for significant others in the immediate community." [11] One of Adler's central ideas supports this relationship between the self and the environment. He believed that man's personality develops in his movement toward a better adaptation to his social and physical environment.[12]

The human being forms his knowledge of himself and the world around him through communication with others. Two systems interact in this process: (1) the social and physical experiences occurring from the interaction of the individual and his immediate environment, usually his family, and (2) the social and physical experiences occurring from the interaction of the individual and the wider society. The less the conflict or difference in the attitudes and interactions between the systems, the more solid the sameness and continuity of identity and the more secure the self-image.

The individual's immediate environment, usually the family, is crucially important in fostering the development of a self that will be able to operate successfully in the wider society. If the young child's needs are reasonably well filled, he sees himself as a worthwhile, lovable being and trusts the world to respond to him on these terms. If the family has emotionally and physically deprived him, he will develop a distrusting attitude toward the world. He will regard himself as a devaluated or worthless object who deserves this type of treatment. Nothing in his experience has informed him that the world can be punitive for reasons that do not involve him or his worth.

Every child thus enters the larger society with some evaluation

[9] Ibid., p. 228.

[10] Erikson, op. cit., p. 19

[11] Ibid., p. 50.

[12] Alfred Adler, op. cit., p. 2.

of self, a self-image derived mostly from communication with his family. In the wider society he continues to be aware of the attitudes of others, to respond to himself as an object, and to develop further evaluations of himself from others' behavior toward him.[13]

BLACK DEVELOPMENT OF SELF

Racial identification, according to a 1947 study by Clark and Clark, appears as early as the third year, and by 7 years, black children cannot escape some racial self-identification and some awareness of the existing cultural attitudes and values attached to race.[14] Recent studies by Morland and Porter indicate that despite the new black consciousness, many black children's racial attitudes about themselves have not changed significantly since the research done by Clark and Clark.[15] Black children still tend to see themselves as devalued compared to white children. Milner hypothesizes that, regardless of the region where he lives or the socioeconomic group to which he belongs, the black child's awareness of his racial group as a socially devalued and differentiated entity increases in emotional impact and complexity as his contacts increase.[16] He begins to understand the negative attitudes of the larger social order toward his own social group, even if he has not experienced them firsthand. The more he incorporates society's negative image into his identity, the more he is devalued in his own image. This is self-destructing rather than self-creating.

To compensate for the potential destruction of self-worth directed from the wider society, blacks incorporate the attitude of two generalized others. The generalized other, as defined by Mead, is the individual assuming the attitude of the wider society.[17] One learns to

---

[13] Mead, op. cit., pp. 135–136.

[14] Kenneth Clark and Mamie Clark, "Racial Identification and Preference in Negro Children," in Theodore H. Newcomb and Eugene L. Hartley, eds., *Readings in Social Psychology* (New York: Henry Holt, 1947), pp. 169–178.

[15] J. Kenneth Morland, "A Comparison of Race-Awareness in Northern and Southern Children," *American Journal of Orthopsychiatry*, 36 (January 1966), pp. 23–31; and Judith Porter, *Black Child, White Child* (Cambridge, Mass.: Harvard University Press, 1971), pp. 111–138.

[16] Esther Milner, "Some Hypotheses Concerning the Influence of Segregation on Negro Personality Development," *Psychiatry*, 16 (August 1953), pp. 291–297.

[17] George H. Mead, *Selected Writings* (Indianapolis, Ind.: Bobbs-Merrill Co., 1964), p. 285.

become an object to oneself, to know oneself through role-taking. In acting out the roles of others the child incorporates them into his own nature and begins to know himself. From the many roles taken on, there gradually arises a sort of generalized other. It is this attitude of the generalized other or organized community attitude that gives unity of self to the individual as he incorporates society's response and reacts accordingly.[18] The black who assumes the attitude of the wider society's generalized other does attain a sense of self, but it is a devaluated and self-destructive self.

MINORITY GENERALIZED OTHER

The alternative generalized other is the attitude of the minority social order—that of the family and immediate community environment. The black child can receive the love and care from his family that can lead to a positive sense of self. Since most blacks are reasonably isolated from the white community both physically and socially, the attitude of the minority generalized other can develop, restore, or help him maintain his self-esteem. He can use it as a buffer against the attitudes of the dominant generalized other. The refuge found in the minority community can never be total, however, because the minority community and the wider society are interdependent. There is constant conflict between the dual generalized others in the maintenance of a positive self-image. Silberman, who supports the idea of a minority generalized other that compensates for the self-devaluation generated by the attitude of the dominant society generalized other, states, "There must be enormously powerful mechanisms of socialization in 'black' subculture to enable people to function in so destructive an environment." [19]

Chestang also speaks of input from two sources, the nurturing environment and the sustaining environment.[20] Chestang's nurturing environment, as he describes it in the essay that appears in this book, is similar to the minority generalized other, and the sustaining environment could be compared to the dominant or majority generalized

[18] Paul E. Pfuetze, *The Social Self* (New York: Bookman Associates, 1954), p. 83.

[19] Charles E. Silberman, *Crisis in Black and White* (New York: Random House, 1964), p. 228.

[20] Leon Chestang, *Character Development in a Hostile Environment*, Occasional Paper No. 3 (Chicago: School of Social Service Administration, University of Chicago, 1972).

other. He believes that the origins of black character cannot be understood until the relationship of these two environments is known. The nurturing environment is the black community and family, where the individual finds emotional support and identity and feels intimacy and being. The sustaining environment houses the goods, services, political power, and economic resources needed by the individual to sustain himself. This is the larger society through which status and power are conferred. When society admits an individual to full participation in both the sustaining and nurturing environments, both merge and the individual becomes a harmonic whole self. If participation in one means exclusion from the other, Chestang believes the individual either accepts an erosion of his humanity or fights it with some energy-consuming adaptive maneuver.

SELF-IMAGE AND GENERALIZED OTHER

The total or overall generalized other of an individual may be thought of as a continuum or series of definitions. attitudes, or expectations with which he perceives himself, the world around him, and his interaction with that world. Both the minority and the majority generalized other can be conceptualized as parts of the total generalized other. Depending on the experience or situation, certain aspects of the generalized other will have primacy or fade into the background.

If both the minority and the majority generalized other reflect the same image of the individual, he incorporates them as a total generalized other without conflict and interacts accordingly. Some individuals receive positive reflections and attitudes from both the minority and majority generalized other, and this leads to a sense of self-worth and harmony in functioning.

There are also individuals with two negative generalized others. This individual's family and immediate community interact with him in a way that denies him self-worth. Coupled with destructive attitudes of the majority generalized other, such a child experiences a lack of self-worth unalleviated by any other perspective. This can lead to the self-hatred phenomenon.

Another set of dynamics is a negative minority generalized other and a positive majority generalized other. An example of this is the child whose immediate contacts offer no positive sense of self-worth but who finds support in the wider society. The attempted incorporation of both of these attitudes would result in conflict. The life experiences of the individual would probably determine which set of attitudes would be dominant. There is a high probability that without the favorable experience from the nurturing environment and a positive self-image the individual may not be able to accept the positive evaluation from the wider society. Expecting rejection, he may act in a manner that assures it, or he may not be able to venture out and take chances in the wider world at all.

The last set of dynamics is the positive sense of self-worth reflected by the minority generalized other and a negative sense reflected by the majority generalized other. This is probably the most common experience of blacks. In this situation the minority generalized other can ameliorate the negative effect of the majority generalized other. In fact, feelings of self-worth in blacks might well depend upon the degree to which the minority generalized other provides perceptions of their experiences that permit someone else other than blacks to be at fault. This underlines the importance of a strong positive minority generalized other to balance the destructive potential of a negative majority generalized other.

SELF-IMAGE AND RESIDENTIAL ENVIRONMENT

The physical and social aspects of the residential environment contribute to the type of minority generalized other an individual develops. The physical part of the residential environment includes all the neighborhood conditions: urban or rural, type of housing, population density in one's home and in the neighborhood as a whole, and the condition of streets and buildings.

The social factors of the residential environment include the mode and type of interaction with one's own family and with people in the immediate neighborhood. The place where a family lives affects the quality of interaction among members of the family. This does not mean that comfortable, adequate housing insures good family relations and poor housing bad ones. Destructive family interactions can occur in any type of residential environment. However, overcrowded, substandard, inadequate housing can strain any type of family interaction. The social factors of the residential environment probably contribute more to the development of positive minority generalized other than the physical factors.

When both the physical and the social factors of the residential environment combine to form negative experiences, the minority generalized other may not be a nurturing set of attitudes. The child whose family destroys his sense of trust and self-worth, who walks filthy hostile streets filled with angry neighbors and gangs who prey on him, often develops an unconscious knowledge that those who live in such squalor cannot be worth much. This message has already been accepted by his family and is a silent attack upon his self-esteem. For a black child in this situation. the majority generalized other is likely to add its negative attitude.

BLACK SELF-IMAGE AND RESIDENTIAL MOVEMENT

The middle-income black has choices in certain domains. His economic status and the partially enforced equal housing laws give him the option of remaining in a segregated residential environment or moving. Preliminary demographic analysis of black residential choices in the Philadelphia area indicates that higher-income blacks who moved within the past several years have not chosen predominantly suburban neighborhoods in nearly the numbers predicted.[21] In his studies of the black middle class, Kronus found that middle-income blacks have historically avoided contact with whites.[22]

Reactions to whites by middle-income blacks follow the lines of acceptance and avoidance. They accept the values of the larger society and pattern their lives to conform to these values. They do not accept the position of inferiority imposed on them by the white society because of the strong sense of self generated by a strong minority generalized other. They tend to avoid contact whenever an imposition of inferiority status may occur. Living in a predominantly white neighborhood risks more frequent occurrence of such encounters.

The purpose of the Philadelphia study was to examine the relationship between black perceptions and experiences and black residential location. Such variables as employment, education, family structure, family residential history, family politics, and the nature of the search for housing, were related to residential choice. Open-ended interviews with a limited number of middle-income black families revealed that they moved to suburbia for concrete advantages such as better schools, lower insurance rates, better municipal services, freedom from gangs molesting their children, better quality food, and access to shopping with parking.[23] Whites probably moved

[21] Cottingham, op. cit., p. 10.

[22] Sidney Kronus, *The Black Middle Class* (Columbus, Ohio: Charles E. Merrill Publishing Co., 1971), p. 11.

[23] Toma Rose Myers, *Black Suburbanization: The Experiences of Seven*

for many or all the same reasons. All the families interviewed felt that they had obtained advantages in their new neighborhoods. None had met open hostility, although some found their neighbors' attitudes "chilly." Myers found that the respondents seemed primarily unconcerned with their neighbors' attitudes.[24]

Factual descriptions of their family life and their friends outside of the community showed these elements to be of more importance to the middle-income blacks' socioemotional well-being than their life within the immediate community. Their major complaint was the disadvantage of commuting back and forth to other neighborhoods to see friends and family and to buy special food products such as "soul food." Their backyard barbecues did not involve neighbors but old friends and family members who were imported for the occasion. The only family who repeatedly expressed concern about its neighbors' coldness had moved into the new neighborhood from another part of the country and had no friends or family in the immediate metropolitan area. They were facing a relatively hostile environment constituting a negative majority generalized other without a supportive environment constituting a positive minority generalized other.

One family that had chosen to remain in the city and fight what the mother called "crime, pollution, congestion, and noise" did so because the father preferred to remain in the "comfortable atmosphere where I grew up, where our family is known and liked and our home is mortgage free."[25] For this family the support received in the immediate residential environment, contributing to a positive minority generalized other, was well worth the physical discomfort of that residential environment.

It is also significant to note that some of the blacks moved to suburban areas where they had previously had positive experiences or had heard of such experiences from other blacks. One family moved to an area where the grandmother had worked as a live-in maid. As a child, the mother had spent summers with the grandmother in the employer's home and had had many pleasant memories of the peaceful atmosphere there. Years later she persuaded her husband to move there from the city to get their teen-age son away from

---

Families, Project Paper (Philadelphia, Pa.: Fels Center of Government, University of Pennsylvania, 1972), p. 11.

[24] Ibid., p. 3

[25] Ibid.

the danger of gangs. The family members still carry on an active social life with family and friends in other areas of the metropolitan area.

These preliminary and limited results appear to support the concept of a dual generalized other. Blacks are aware of the negative attitude of the wider society. However, its impact on their self-image is tempered by the adoption of the attitude of the significant other, usually black, in the immediate community. The sense of self-worth emanating from a positive minority generalized other permits them to operate in the white world, take advantage of its opportunities, and not undergo destruction of the self.

There appears to be a relationship between the way black people view themselves and where they live. Some blacks may contribute to the continuing pattern of segregation because their experiences with racism cause them to protect their self-esteem by avoiding residence in a white neighborhood. Other blacks with a strong concept of self grown out of the new emphasis on black identity may prefer to live in a black residential area.

IMPLICATIONS FOR HOUSING POLICY

Major government policies designed to improve housing opportunities for blacks stress the elimination of racial discrimination among realtors and lending agencies and push for open housing legislation. Despite this, blacks still live in predominantly black residential environments. Some federal and local policies have attempted to provide subsidized moderate-income housing in predominantly white communities, but this has usually not proved successful.[26]

Successful open housing policy may not be feasible in the short term for three major reasons:

1. Present housing policy has no widely effective programs for altering entrenched white attitudes against having blacks in certain communities. Kantrowitz in his study of housing segregation in New York, which appears in this volume, states that housing policy is ineffective because people will always tend to cluster around people of the same race and socioeconomic class. If Kantrowitz's hypothesis of voluntary segregation is true, then housing policies directed toward a goal of socioeconomic and racial heterogeneity may be unrealistic.

---

[26] "Federal Government's Role in the Achievement of Equal Opportunity in Housing," op. cit.

2. Some blacks may prefer to live in an all-black environment out of a need to avoid the assaults against their self-image almost inevitable in predominantly white communities.

3. Other blacks may prefer an all-black residential environment because of their commitment to a strong black identification.

Despite such obstacles to residential mixing, some blacks and whites prefer or would accept integrated housing and think open housing policies should continue. Integrated housing should not, however, be the major thrust of housing policy.

PERSONALITY ISSUES AND HOUSING POLICY

Housing policy should be considered in relation to issues of personality: (1) a positive self-image is desirable, for it implies healthier, freer people more likely to develop their full potential, (2) the self-image develops as a result of the interactions between the individual and the attitudes of the immediate environment (the minority generalized other) and of the larger society (the majority generalized other), (3) the minority generalized other (especially that of minorities) needs to be strong and positive in order to develop a healthy self-image, and (4) the residential environment composed of the immediate physical and social environments contributes to the development of the minority generalized other and the individual. Thus, housing policy should focus on those factors in the residential environment that contribute to a strong minority generalized other.

Substandard, overcrowded housing, filthy and dangerous streets, inadequate and scarred school buildings staffed with teachers who do not understand their pupils—all these are attacks on positive self-image. Housing policy should address these problems by providing decent housing, clean streets with regular trash pick-ups and sweeping, adequately lighted and patrolled streets, and ample playground and recreational facilities. All groups should have these and other services in their residential environment regardless of race or socioeconomic status. Housing policies should be geared toward improving the quality of urban neighborhood services wherever people choose or feel obliged to live.

Perhaps "housing" policy implies too narrow a focus, and the goal should be "residential" policy. This should include education, health, transportation, and security services. The quality and convenience of housing and residential services in all neighborhoods, especially low income ones, should have as high a priority as the achievement of open housing.

A report to the Department on Housing and Urban Development (HUD) by the Social Science Panel of the National Academy of Sciences appears to support this dual emphasis. The report states that HUD must be as concerned with the equitable distribution of services as with the access to housing.[27]

Neither segregated housing nor opposition to residential mixing is advocated here. Housing options for minorities should be increased, but concentrated effort to improve the quality of housing and services wherever people live may prove to be a realistic and effective second major goal for housing policy. Politically, it could be feasible since politicians are less likely to be attacked on the spending issue if everyone is receiving the services. However, economically, there could be a problem in urban areas with dwindling tax bases. Like most social policy, priorities may have to be set among the services provided.

Social policies that maximize the positive effect on as many ethnic, racial, and socioeconomic groups as possible would be the best policies for the total society. A focus on comprehensive residential services would be an effective social policy because it would encourage the fulfillment of human potential.

[27] Amos H. Hawley and Vincent P. Peck, eds., *Segregation in Residential Areas* (Washington, D.C.: National Academy of Science, 1973), p. 19.

part three

ETHNICITY ISSUES FOR SOCIAL POLICY

Transitional Values of Puerto Ricans

JOSEPH FITZPATRICK

Joseph Fitzpatrick, Ph.D., is Professor of Sociology, Fordham University, Bronx, New York.

EDITORS' COMMENT

Puerto Ricans comprise the last large-scale migration into American cities. An examination of their ethnic cultural patterns and their assimilation into American society shows why social policy must be responsive to different ethnic communities. Family educational patterns are most revealing in their implications for social policy.

The emphasis by the Puerto Rican community on bilingual education combines the legal concept of equality of educational opportunity with that of cultural survival and retention of ethnic identity. Traditionally, public education has been a means of socialization and assimilation. But with the establishment of bilingual education programs by the state of New York, the notion of equal educational opportunity for all is placed in the context of ethnic group culture.

A number of policies and programs in New York City have been particularly effective. They were designed to serve a particular culture and have been administered by people who understand that culture. Acknowledging ethnic group culture in creating public policy is important, but such policies must not bind those forging a new identity to the old immigrant culture. It is evident that the Puerto Rican community is in a process of change and adaptation to American society. The rate, for example, of intermarriage among Puerto Ricans in New York is presently as high as it was for all immigrant groups in New York from 1908–14. Social policy must acknowledge such change.

Seventy-five years ago Puerto Rico became part of the United States. It was about fifty years ago that the first substantial group of Puerto Ricans began to settle in New York City, but the large-scale migration to the mainland did not begin in earnest until after World War II. The 1970 Census reported 817,712 persons of Puerto Rican birth and parentage in New York City: 473,300 (58 percent) of these were born in Puerto Rico; 344,412 (42 percent) were born on the mainland of Puerto Rican parentage.[1] In other words, almost half the Puerto Rican population in New York City is second generation. In this context it would seem that the Puerto Rican population should be "coming of age" as New Yorkers, manifesting that maturity which one associates with a people who have begun to establish themselves solidly in a new land.

There is evidence of that maturity and self-confidence. As of 1975 Puerto Ricans had an elected congressman in Washington, a senator and three assemblymen in the New York State Legislature, and two elected city councilmen in New York City. A Puerto Rican had been president of the Board of Higher Education of New York for four years, and the seven-member Board of Education had a Puerto Rican serving on it. One of the top officials of the Board of Education was a Puerto Rican. There were nineteen Puerto Rican principals in the schools in contrast to five in 1969. In addition, a Puerto Rican was serving as a special assistant to the mayor. In terms of elected and

[1] U.S. Department of Commerce, Bureau of the Census, *1970 Census of Population: Subject Reports, Puerto Ricans in the United States,* PC(2)–1E (Washington, D.C., U.S. Government Printing Office, 1973), p. xi.

appointed officials, the Puerto Rican community was decidedly in evidence.

There are also solid and effective grass-roots organizations: Aspira in the area of education; the Puerto Rican Family Institute in the area of social service; the Puerto Rican Forum functioning in a wide range of social, economic, and public activities; the Puerto Rican Travelling Theatre and El Museo del Barrio in the arts; and the Puerto Rican Merchants' Association for proprietors of small businesses. The list could go on and on. In view of all this, the ordinary observer would be inclined to say the Puerto Ricans have arrived.

But there is other evidence that things are not going so well. The Puerto Rican population is still the poorest by far in New York City. According to the 1970 census, median family income for Puerto Ricans was $5,575. This was $1,757 lower than that of the black population. While median real family income for the black population increased from 1960 to 1970 by 26 percent, the median real family income of the Puerto Ricans increased by only 13 percent. In 1970, 30.4 percent of the Puerto Rican families had annual incomes below the poverty level, compared to 20.4 percent of the blacks and 11.5 percent of the total population.[2]

More serious yet, there is little evidence of any significant improvement among second-generation Puerto Ricans. In education the picture continues to be bleak. In 1970, the dropout rate among Puerto Ricans between the beginning of high school and the end was 61 percent. Puerto Rican districts continue to have the lowest scores in reading and mathematics of all pupils in New York State. In 1970, 25.5 percent of all addicts under treatment in New York State were Puerto Ricans; 82 percent of these were high school dropouts.[3]

In view of this, it is important to ask why. How does one reconcile the evidence of steady advancement with the evidence of continuing failure? Are there policies that are responsible for this disadvantaged condition? Are there policies that could correct it? An examination of two areas of central importance, education and the family, might shed some light on the central issue and indicate the manner in which public policy has been and will continue to be related to the Puerto Rican experience.

[2] *A Socio-Economic Profile of Puerto Rican New Yorkers*, Regional Report 46 (New York: U.S. Department of Labor, Bureau of Labor Statistics, Middle Atlantic Regional Office, July 1975), pp. 106–111.

[3] Regents of the University of the State of New York, *Bilingual Education* (Albany, N.Y.: State Department of Education, June 1972).

POPULATION SIZE

Numbers are important. The Puerto Ricans in New York City have not yet reached the two million mark that other ethnic groups, such as the Irish, the Jews, the Italians, have reached and that blacks will soon reach. But two things may result in a substantial increase in numbers: a recurrence of large-scale migration of Puerto Ricans to New York City and a continued high rate of reproduction among them.

Puerto Ricans, as American citizens, are free to move anywhere they wish to go. Their migration is largely motivated by a desire to increase their income and thus responds to economic conditions in Puerto Rico and New York.

The second factor of reproduction is much more likely to affect gross population size. From a simple demographic point of view, the reproductive potential of the Puerto Ricans is extraordinary. About 50 percent of the first-generation Puerto Ricans in the United States were under 21 years of age in 1970, and almost 84 percent of the second generation were under 21. Nearly half the Puerto Ricans are now second generation.[4] When these large numbers marry and have families, even small families, they will have an enormous impact on the population of New York City. In a future generation they may reach the size of the previous large ethnic groups in the city. The liberal New York State abortion law may affect this increase, although no reliable evidence about the extent to which Puerto Rican women are seeking abortions has been made public. But a high birth rate is not necessary in order to have a substantial numerical increase.

EDUCATION

Puerto Ricans in New York City consider education to be a major area of crisis. Current policy issues that focus on the changing concept of culture and its relation to education have resulted in some dramatic improvements, but these same issues may become complicated in the future.

The major complaint of the Puerto Ricans during the past twenty years has been that their children are not being educated. In the fall of 1974, there were 253,452 Puerto Ricans in the public schools of

---

[4] *1970 Census of Population: Subject Reports, Puerto Ricans in the United States,* op. cit., Table 2.

New York City, 23 percent of the total enrollment.[5] As indicated earlier, they have the highest high school dropout rate and the lowest reading and math scores. Previously this was a handicap to entering college, but the higher education scene is now more favorable. In the fall of 1974, there were 16,352 Puerto Ricans in the City University of New York. They represented 7.4 percent of the total enrollment, an increase of 3.4 percent since 1969. They have advanced from 2.9 percent in the senior colleges in 1969 to 6.3 percent in 1974.[6]

The major policy issue at the elementary and high school levels has been bilingual education. The major policy issue for higher education had been open admission until the city's financial crisis in 1976 resulted in the termination of the City University's open admissions program. A number of additional issues are potentially even more explosive and emotional. A debate centers around the concept of pluralism in American society and the extent to which the schools should adapt to the cultural styles and needs of newcomers. Conversely, the question also involves how the schools should prepare Puerto Rican students to move into the social, cultural, economic, and political mainstream of American life.

This can be clarified by a look at the changing concept of culture as it has affected bilingual education, compensatory education, and the demand for teachers who share the same culture as their students. All these issues converge sharply around the critical problem of jobs, and the criteria for selecting among applicants. As in all issues touching immigrant groups, the problem of competition for jobs in the educational system may come to overshadow all other educational issues.

Bilingual education. The first major effort to examine the experience of Puerto Ricans in the schools of New York was *The Puerto Rican Study, 1953–57,* an extensive study funded by the Ford Foundation to identify the problems of Puerto Rican children in the schools and to suggest remedies.[7] A central focus of the study was language. There was a strong recommendation for bilingual programs, but the pur-

[5] *Ethnic Census of the School Population* (New York: Board of Education of the City of New York, October 1974).

[6] *Percentage of Puerto Rican and other Spanish Surnamed Undergraduate Students* (New York: City University of New York, Office of Data Collection and Evaluation, April 1974).

[7] *The Puerto Rican Study, 1953–1957* (New York: Board of Education of the City of New York, 1958.)

pose of bilingual programs recommended by the study was to accelerate the learning of English so that the child could perform well in an English-speaking environment.

Ten years after this study was completed, the first city-wide Puerto Rican conference took place. Many participants were discouraged: despite the recommendations of the Puerto Rican study, the situation since 1957 had become worse. Attention again focused on bilingual education, but the concept was extended. Bilingual education should not only help Puerto Rican children learn English more effectively; it should also help Puerto Rican culture survive, a value of increasing importance among all Puerto Ricans. Bilingual education in general, and Puerto Rican studies in particular, were seen as means of enabling Puerto Rican youth to remain rooted in their own heritage while growing up in their new environment. The first completely bilingual schools were started in New York City in 1968.

Inherent in the establishment of the bilingual schools was the educational philosophy that a child from a Spanish-speaking home will learn English much more rapidly if he first learns the Spanish language native to him. If the child reads and writes well in Spanish, he will transfer this skill readily to English. But the significant thing from the viewpoint of values and policy was not this educational theory. It was the concept of bilingualism as a means to preserve the culture of Puerto Rican children. This became the emphasis in the late 1960s.

In June 1972, the Regents of the University of the State of New York formally adopted a policy of bilingual education. The policy was seen as a requirement if equality in education was to be achieved.

> A fundamental tenet of bilingual education is that a person living in a society whose language and culture differ from his own must be equipped to participate meaningfully in the mainstream of that society. It should not be necessary for him to sacrifice his rich native language and culture to achieve such participation. Rather, we should utilize available language skills and thought processes to foster intellectual development while developing English language proficiency. The purpose of this position paper is to direct concerted and effective action toward achieving this end.[8]

Thus, the concept of cultural survival and continuity converged with the powerful legal concept of equality of educational opportunity. The end result was the official policy of bilingual education.

However, official policy statements did not settle the issue. In

---

[8] Regents of the University of the State of New York, op. cit., p. 7.

1972, on behalf of Aspira, a Puerto Rican organization dedicated to promoting educational opportunities for Puerto Rican children, the Puerto Rican Legal Defense and Education Fund brought suit in the courts demanding bilingual education as a civil right. The theory guiding this action is clearly stated in the Fund's report:

> The Fund is committed to insuring that each Puerto Rican child enjoys the equal educational opportunity that is due all citizens. In a suit entitled *Aspira* v. *Board of Education* filed on behalf of the more than 182,000 Puerto Rican and other Hispanic school children in New York City, the Fund has charged that teaching non-English-speaking children in a language they do not understand violates their constitutional rights. The suit demands that Spanish-speaking children learn their substantive subjects in Spanish while being taught English. Such a bilingual program would also expose children to the history and culture of the Hispanic people.[9]

The policy issues around bilingualism will increase in complexity during the coming decade for a number of reasons. The identification of children who are to be taught "subjects" in Spanish is becoming difficult. The number of non-Puerto Rican Hispanics is increasing rapidly in New York City schools. In the fall of 1974, there were 54,392 such children enrolled. Obviously, the cultural background of a Cuban is different from that of a Puerto Rican, as is that of an Ecuadorian or a person from Santo Domingo. The presentation of varied subject matter adapted to the specific cultures of these various Hispanic groups will be difficult and complicated. In addition, large numbers of Puerto Rican parents resist the concept of bilingual education altogether. Preoccupied with economic survival and advancement, they want to be sure that their children will be competent in English.

The major problem, however, will be found among the Puerto Ricans born or raised in New York City. In 1970 they constituted 42 percent of the Puerto Rican population. These are the so-called "Newyoricans," many of whom are now returning to Puerto Rico. In 1973–74, 10,771 children transferred from public schools in New York City to schools in Puerto Rico.[10] Linguistically and culturally,

[9] *First Annual Report, 1972–1973* (New York: Puerto Rican Legal Defense and Education Fund, p. 9).

[10] *Transfers of Public School Students between Puerto Rico and New York City, 1954 Through 1973* (New York: Board of Education of the City of New York, Bureau of Attendance, Spring, 1974).

they are different from island Puerto Ricans. Many do not know enough Spanish to perform well in school. They are frequently stigmatized as second-class Puerto Ricans. The increasing number of problems related to the Newyoricans is causing widespread concern on the island.

Young Puerto Ricans in New York are also searching for an identity, for they are neither conventional New Yorkers nor traditional Puerto Ricans. There is considerable pathos in the posture of many young Puerto Ricans who criticize the cultural imperialism of the United States and campaign for the independence of the island and the preservation of its traditional culture, but who repudiate much of the Puerto Rican culture in their own lives. An interesting literature is emerging that reflects some of the turmoil young Puerto Ricans are experiencing.[11]

The implications of this for policy are not at all clear. Although an intelligent and imaginative presentation of their Puerto Rican background may become an ordinary part of mainland instruction, the culture they preserve will not be purely Puerto Rican. An educational policy that seeks to provide instruction for children of different cultural backgrounds in the context of each child's culture is a policy no one faults. But to carry it out effectively in the midst of the cultural turmoil that Puerto Ricans face will be a difficult and aggravating task.

Compensatory education. The issue of whether educational institutions would help each ethnic group maintain its own culture has also become important in the area of compensatory education. In this form the issue involves not only Puerto Ricans. It gets to the heart of the basic definition of cultural pluralism and calls into question the traditional function of the public school to socialize the child into the dominant culture of the United States. Its influence on educational theory and policy has already been significant. It will become more so in the next decade.

Earlier theories that explained the failure of children to achieve in school as a manifestation of inherited inferiority are now unpopular and controversial.[12] It became much more common after World War

---

[11] *See,* for example, Samuel Betances, ed., *The Rican: Journal of Contemporary Puerto Rican Thought,* published in Chicago beginning in 1971; and José Angel Figueroa, *East 110th Street* (Detroit, Mich.: Broadside Press, 1973).

[12] Arthur R. Jensen, "How Much Can We Boost IQ and Scholastic Achievement?" *Harvard Education Review,* 39 (1969), pp. 1–123 and 449–483.

II to explain such failure by attributing it to "cultural deprivation." This meant simply that people from minority cultures were often ill-prepared to manage the process of learning in a modern, predominantly middle-class school system. Compensatory education was perceived as a method of providing the child with those skills and ways of thinking that would enable him to perform better in a system that was culturally foreign to him. It was a process of intensive resocialization. This position was also challenged.

The importance of cultural differences began to be stressed. Specific strengths and values in individual cultures were recognized as having a right to survive and develop.[13] This resulted in extensive criticism of modern schooling as an oppressive process in which one culture smothers the authentic values and strengths of other cultures. Stodolsky and Lesser called attention to the implications of this theory: If "disadvantaged" means occupying a low social class position, it is possible to follow the strategy of giving the "have-nots" what the "haves" possess. If, on the other hand, "disadvantaged" is defined to mean differences in ethnic group membership, it is no longer possible to follow that strategy.[14] Ethnicity cannot be changed by money, social degree, or compensatory programs. The point of providing equal opportunity to everyone is not to equalize development, as was emphasized in the Coleman Report, but to enable each ethnic group to realize more fully its own native qualities, even if this means the continuation of ethnic differences among the groups.[15] Thus compensatory education inevitably raises the problem of cultural pluralism. As the author has expressed it elsewhere:

> The issue of cultural pluralism around schooling, therefore, remains fundamental. Policy decisions concerning this issue will directly affect educational strategies, and educational experience will directly influence policy. Are there common cultural features which all people living in the United States must share if they are not going to be seriously deprived within this environment? If not, what educational policies must be adopted in order to enable people to retain their specific cultural background if they wish? If yes, what educational policies must be

[13] See, for example, Frank Riessman, The Culturally Deprived Child (New York: Harper and Row, 1962).

[14] Susan S. Stodolsky and Gerald Lesser, "Learning Patterns in the Disadvantaged," Harvard Educational Review, 37 (Fall 1967) p. 573.

[15] James S. Coleman et al., Equality of Educational Opportunity (Washington, D.C.: U.S Department of Health, Education and Welfare, Office of Education, 1966), especially pp. 21–23.

adopted to form school children in that culture, despite the different mental abilities and behavioral skills in which their families have already formed them? Compensatory education, to be effective, must be defined in relation to these major issues of policy and strategy, and the way the decisions are made will have a major influence on the identity of the Puerto Ricans.[16]

Cultural compatibility. A troubling consequence of the previous two issues is this question: Who will teach Puerto Rican children if instruction in Spanish becomes a fixed policy and if the culture of Puerto Rican children is to be preserved in the midst of the mainland culture? This problem manifests itself on two levels. There is first a theoretical level. Many social scientists are emphasizing that only insiders can really understand other insiders. This means that only blacks can accurately study black people and only Puerto Ricans can fully understand and communicate with Puerto Rican people.[17]

More emotional still is the practical level of service. Only insiders are capable of providing educational, social, and medical services to other insiders. This theory has emerged from abundant evidence that, in many cases, professionals serving people from a minority group misinterpreted their needs or misdirected services to them. They misunderstood the cultural cues that would have been clear to a person of the same cultural background as the client.[18] Extensive efforts have been made to overcome this problem through the use of paraprofessionals, but the demand continues that blacks be appointed to serve blacks and Puerto Ricans be appointed to serve Puerto Ricans.

This has created a serious controversy over the policies that direct the appointment of teachers, principals, and educational officials. Should the basis of competency be established through supposedly objective tests with universal norms or tests using the particularistic norms of ethnic or racial identity? The cry "reverse discrimination" has become loud not only in New York City but across the nation.

---

[16] Joseph P. Fitzpatrick, *Puerto Rican Americans: The Meaning of Migration to the Mainland* (Englewood Cliffs, N.J.: Prentice-Hall, 1971), p. 141.

[17] *See* Robert K. Merton, "Insiders and Outsiders," *Varieties of Political Expression in Sociology* (Chicago: University of Chicago Press, 1972), pp. 9–47.

[18] For the situation in mental health, *see* Joseph P. Fitzpatrick and Robert E. Gould, M.D., "Mental Illness Among Puerto Ricans in New York: Cultural Condition or Intercultural Misunderstanding?" in Ben Rubenstein and Martin Levitt, eds., *On the Urban Scene* (Detroit, Mich.: Wayne State University Press, 1972), pp. 48–64.

The Antidefamation League of the B'nai B'rith has complained that less qualified blacks and Puerto Ricans are being appointed as principals or assistant principals while more qualified candidates are being passed over.[19] The United Federation of Teachers, which has a strong Jewish constituency, carefully scrutinizes appointments made by the decentralized school boards and is ready to protest if official norms are not observed and preference is shown to blacks and Puerto Ricans.

This issue will certainly become a matter of increasing controversy if public policy continues to shift in favor of the ethnic and racial minorities. In 1971, a federal judge restrained the Board of Education of the City of New York from appointing principals on the basis of tests given by the Board of Examiners, a policy that had been in force for many years. He held that appointment according to this method resulted in obvious discrimination: only eleven black principals and one Puerto Rican principal (a combined total of 1.4 percent) had been appointed at a time when 55 percent of the entire public school system consisted of black and Puerto Rican children.[20]

In the area of social service, the concept of service being provided by people who thoroughly understand a particular culture has had some sensational results. In 1972 the Department of Social Services negotiated a contract with the Puerto Rican Family Institute to provide family support services to Spanish-speaking families with children who were about to be placed in public or private institutions. During the first year, out of 125 families with 600 children served by the institute, placement was necessary for only two children. The rest were able to stay at home with their families.[21]

This kind of success will certainly have its impact on agency policy in the next few years. But it will not be without its conflicts and dangers. The policy of service within a particular culture by people who understand that culture is beginning to be challenged as a violation of civil rights by people who are highly qualified according to standardized norms.

An even more complicated issue arises around the need to define who is a minority member and who is not. At what point does a group cease to be a minority and lose the right to be compensated

---

[19] *See New York Times,* July 16, 1974.

[20] *New York Times,* July 15, 1974.

[21] *Report on Placement Prevention* (New York: Puerto Rican Family Institute, June 1974).

for the disadvantage of that status? In 1973, a complaint was brought before the state Human Rights Commission against the New York State Department of Labor by an Italian girl. She charged that she had been dismissed from her job and replaced by a member of a "minority" group because the department was required to pursue a policy of affirmative action. The commission cautioned the Department of Labor about discrimination.[22]

Concern for the cultural differences of ethnic groups will therefore continue to be a major influence on policy in New York City. It is most important in those situations in which cultural similarity or cultural insight leads to confidence and understanding between one who provides public service and one who receives it. It is also important in helping newcomers retain a sense of identity or achieve a new sense of identity by cultivating in them a knowledge of and respect for the culture from which they come. It will result in complications and controversy if it implies the perpetuation of a culture among youths who are forging a new culture and a new identity, or if one culture appears to be favored more than another. Basic policy questions will be determined by the manner in which cultural pluralism is defined, and serious conflicts of interest will continue around the question of appointment to positions on the basis of objectively established competence rather than ethnic or racial identity.

THE FAMILY

Moynihan has always questioned why the United States has no family policy.[23] Clearly one is needed, but in view of the profound cultural changes in the United States today, there is little likelihood that one will be forthcoming. Almost every aspect of policy affects the family in some way, but it is in the area of their implications for family life that policy questions quickly become controversial.

With reference to the Puerto Ricans, some basic data reveal the areas that can easily become related to policy. According to the 1970 census, 28 percent of the Puerto Rican heads of families in the

---

[22] *New York Times,* June 28, 1974, p. 35.

[23] Daniel P. Moynihan, *The Negro Family: The Case for National Action* (Washington, D.C.: U.S. Department of Labor, Office of Policy Planning and Research, March 1965), especially Chap. 5.

New York City Standard Metropolitan Statistical Area were female. This statistic becomes more dramatic when the data for the second generation are examined. Almost 26 percent of second-generation Puerto Rican family heads are female, considerably more than the 18.5 percent in Puerto Rico.[24] Whatever this phenomenon means, there is little evidence that it is tapering off in the second generation. These statistics must be examined in the light of the demographic data presented earlier, namely that 50 percent of the first generation and more than 87 percent of the second generation were below 21 years of age in 1970. If the pattern of female-headed families continues to be high in the second generation, the numbers both of children and mothers involved in this type of family will increase substantially. If so, it probably will receive much more attention than it is receiving now. Unfortunately, the phenomenon of female-headed families is not well understood. Nor does much reliable information exist about its effect on Puerto Rican children or on the Puerto Rican community. Furthermore, this is an area that encompasses values, religious beliefs and practices, and profound questions concerning the nature of marriage, family, and sexual relationships.

Among poor families in Puerto Rico, as with poor families throughout the Caribbean, the female-headed family is not unusual. But in Puerto Rico at the present time the rate is lower than among Puerto Ricans in the New York area. The extent to which the rate in New York City may be related to public welfare is questionable. Does the convenient absence of the father from the home make it easier for the wife to receive Aid to Families with Dependent Children? Puerto Ricans resent this suggestion, and the Department of Social Services in New York regularly denies that welfare cheating takes place on so large a scale. Perhaps the availability of welfare results in a much more casual abandonment of a family by the husband, or separation of husband and wife. Does the Moynihan thesis apply, namely, that the Puerto Rican man, like the black man, leaves his family when it becomes impossible to provide adequate economic support for them? No one has a satisfactory or convincing answer.

Whatever the explanation, the female-headed family is predominantly a family receiving public assistance. According to a New York State Department of Welfare study in May 1969, 40 percent of all families receiving Aid to Dependent Children in New York City were

[24] *1970 Census of Population: Subject Reports, Puerto Ricans in the United States,* PC(2)–1E, op. cit., Table 5.

Puerto Rican families.[25] But the problem of poverty among Puerto Ricans goes far beyond the female-headed family. It must be remembered that the Puerto Ricans are by far the poorest segment of New York's population. Thirty percent of the Puerto Rican families were below the poverty level in 1970. Therefore, welfare policy becomes a critical issue in relation to them. The failure of the national government to adopt a policy of income maintenance and the veto in December 1971 by President Richard M. Nixon of the bill for day care centers have had serious consequences in New York. Because it has the most generous welfare benefits in the nation and because most Puerto Ricans live there, New York State bears an excessive financial burden. The failure to expand the day care center program leaves many Puerto Rican women with no alternative but welfare since they have no place to leave their children when they work.

New York City has been trying to improve its welfare policies and administration for many years. It becomes increasingly clear that little can be done in the area of welfare unless more effective policies affecting employment are developed. The city is presently at the mercy of national and international economic factors that no particular city policy can easily influence.

Two other aspects of family life can be briefly mentioned. In 1969, close to 30 percent of all Puerto Rican births in New York City were out-of-wedlock births. This represents a steady increase from 11 percent in 1957, to 22 percent in 1967, to 30 percent in 1969.[26] Such births are not unusual in Puerto Rico, where many couples, especially among the poor, live together for long periods but do not marry. Births to mothers who are living consensually would be registered as out-of-wedlock in New York, but in the context of Puerto Rican culture, the out-of-wedlock child is received in a much kindlier fashion than in middle-class America. They are regularly welcomed into the family of the unwed mother. For sociological reasons, it would be helpful to have some way of distinguishing a child born to a woman after a casual union from a child born to a woman in a stable but consensual union. The new liberal abortion laws of New York State may have a significant influence on the birthrate of out-of-wedlock chil-

---

[25] *The Administration of Aid to Families with Dependent Children in New York City, November 1968–February 1969.* Report of a joint review carried out by the U.S. Department of Health, Education and Welfare and New York State Department of Social Services, September 1969.

[26] Department of Statistics and Analysis, New York City Health Service Administration.

dren, but no readily available data exist about the extent to which Puerto Rican women are seeking abortions.

One final observation about Puerto Rican families is important. According to the 1970 census, there is a strong trend toward outgroup marriage in the second generation. Among first-generation men, 11 percent had wives who were not Puerto Rican; among the second generation, it was 33 percent. Among first-generation women, 11 percent had husbands who were not Puerto Rican; among second-generation women, it was 30 percent.[27] This supports the author's data on outgroup marriage among Puerto Ricans in New York between 1950 and 1960.[28] It is the same rate as that for all immigrant groups in New York City from 1908 to 1914. This indicates that Puerto Ricans are intermingling with Americans of other ethnic groups to a significant degree. If this pattern continues, it will deeply affect Puerto Rican culture on the mainland. It indicates that an old and familiar human pattern may yet make a wide range of public policy unnecessary. Therefore, the important policies with regard to the Puerto Rican family will be those related to welfare.

[27] *1970 Census of Population: Subject Reports, Puerto Ricans in the United States,* PC(2)–1E, op. cit., Table 5.

[28] Fitzpatrick, op. cit., p. 95.

Immigration, Work Expectations, and Labor Market Structure

MICHAEL J. PIORE

Michael J. Piore, Ph.D., is Professor, Department of Economics, Massachusetts Institute of Technology, Cambridge, Massachusetts. This study was supported by a grant from the Manpower Administration, U.S. Department of Labor, Washington, D.C. The Manpower Administration, however, assumes no responsibility for its contents.

EDITORS' COMMENT

The process of ethnic assimilation is closely related to that of economic assimilation. As Greeley has shown, there is a long history of migration to the United States, particularly to its urban areas. For the European immigrant, the process has lasted for more than a century. Fitzpatrick has shown how racial factors have complicated the assimilation of the most recent immigrants.

Using the dual labor-market hypothesis, Piore highlights the socioeconomic factor of immigrant assimilation. On the basis of his case study of Puerto Rican workers in Boston, Piore identifies three key elements influencing the migration: (1) a set of dead-end jobs that the native labor force will not accept, (2) a new immigrant population with a labor-market perspective molded in an underdeveloped region where these jobs are acceptable, and (3) a second generation that is descended from some earlier migrant stream that was originally recruited to fill these jobs but that has come to adopt the perspective of the natives. Since it appears that the economy can neither function without the migrant stream nor prevent the migrants from settling and producing a second generation, it is clear that public policy should focus on opening the channels for upward mobility that correspond to the expectations of a second generation.

This essay develops two basic propositions: (1) a continuous stream of migrants from economically backward areas is critical to the process of economic growth as it has occurred in the Western world, and (2) the social tensions associated with ethnic and racial minorities which both the United States and Western European nations have been experiencing in recent years are a by-product of this migratory process and the particular ways in which it has been organized in modern times. These propositions are derived from a case study of the migration of Puerto Rican workers to Boston, Massachusetts. That study was in turn conceived within the framework of the dual labor-market hypothesis.

DUAL LABOR-MARKET HYPOTHESIS

The dual labor-market hypothesis was developed in the middle of the 1960s in reaction to the then prevailing diagnosis of the employment problems of the black ghettos in the central cities.[1] That diagnosis focused on the high levels of unemployment and the "unemployability" of the central-city population. The causes were frequently

[1] See David Gordon, *Theories of Poverty and Unemployment* (Lexington, Mass.: D. C. Heath & Co., 1972), pp. 43–52.

traced to the growing technical sophistication demanded by the job market and the lagging educational facilities of the rural areas where much of the central city population was thought to have originated. However, a number of facets of the economic life of the ghetto seemed to conflict with this view. Most prominent among them were these socioeconomic conditions: employer complaints of labor shortage; high turnover rates among ghetto workers; the prevalent belief that anybody who really wanted to work could find employment; and the fact that urban discontent seemed to be positively correlated with education and industrial sophistication.

The dual labor-market hypothesis attempts to explain these contradictions in terms of a fundamental dichotomy of the labor market into a primary and a secondary sector. Work in ghetto areas appears to form part of a secondary sector, with jobs distinguished from primary jobs by a series of characteristics: low wages, poor working conditions, instability and insecurity of employment, lack of opportunity for advancement, and a personal (as opposed to institutional) relationship between the supervisor and subordinate. These characteristics are basically antagonistic to those of primary jobs. They reward traits resembling those rewarded by illicit activity and by the welfare system and make it relatively easy for workers to move back and forth among these three income-distributing systems. The central problem of ghetto labor markets, then, is that such secondary jobs predominate and that ghetto workers are confined to them and to activities which resemble them and do not have access to positions in the primary sector. The high unemployment rates are thus viewed as derivative of the short duration of the jobs and the high rates of voluntary employee turnover which that encourages.

Since the formulation of this view, most of its proponents have attempted to incorporate it into a broader theory of labor market stratification and economic mobility.[2] These efforts are not of great significance in the current context, but two revisions are noteworthy. One uses intragenerational mobility as the focus of a theory of labor market stratification and identifies the lack of opportunities for upward mobility as the basic characteristic distinguishing the secondary

[2] Michael J. Piore, *Notes for a Theory of Labor Market Stratification*, Working Paper No. 95 (Cambridge, Mass.: MIT Department of Economics, 1972); and Michael Reich, David M. Gordon, and Richard E. Edwards, "A Theory of Labor Market Segmentation," and Thomas Vietorisz and Bennett Harrison, "A Theory of Sub-employment and the Labor Market," *American Economic Review*, 63 (May 1973), pp. 359–376.

sector. The other amendment points out that the labor force in the secondary sector is composed of disadvantaged workers, youth, and women and that the jobs in this sector seem particularly suited to the needs of youth and are not symptomatic of the more fundamental social pathology they seem to represent for ethnic and racial minorities.

Migration—and the role of employers in encouraging it—has been noted in earlier studies of the dual labor-market hypothesis.[3] It is of special interest for several reasons. First, migration was one factor confirming employer assertions about labor shortage, which the conventional wisdom would have attributed to employer prejudice and bigotry. Second, the migrants sought by employers seemed to be largely unschooled. This seemed to contradict the accepted belief that educational requirements were rising, rendering the uneducated unemployable. Third, the migration process appeared to offer an insight into the dynamics of low-income labor markets which had until that time been viewed largely in static terms.

Puerto Rican migration to Boston is particularly interesting because it seems to have arisen suddenly, the population growing from almost zero in the middle sixties to become a significant component of the central-city population by 1971. The recent origins of the process made it possible to identify its root causes and its dynamics in the initial stages.

PUERTO RICAN MIGRATION INTO BOSTON

The case study reported on here used a series of initial interviews, conducted with strategically placed community leaders and professional employees of community-based labor market and welfare institutions. Respondents were asked to discuss the nature of the migration process and the employment patterns among the migrant population. They were also asked to identify firms in the area with heavy concentrations of Puerto Rican employees. These firms were contacted and extensive interviews were conducted with their managerial personnel. In some community projects and at a few work sites, interviews were also conducted with the migrants themselves, but no systematic attempt was made to pursue this line of inquiry.

[3] Michael J. Piore, "Jobs and Training," in Samuel H. Beer and Richard E. Barringer, eds., *The State and the Poor* (Cambridge, Mass.: Winthrop Publishers, 1970), p. 61.

Impressions gathered through these various types of interviews were compared with data drawn from the 1970 census and from two special surveys of the Spanish-speaking populations in Boston, one of which included other ethnic groups.[4] The mobility of the Puerto Rican population gave rise to serious sampling biases in all three of these data sources, including the census, but these biases were less serious since the sources were used in combination with and as a check against the interviews. Experiences of the investigators in Puerto Rico and with black migrants in Northern central cities and in the rural South constituted the final input into the study.

The census shows a growth of the Spanish-speaking population in Boston from less than one thousand in 1959 to over seventeen thousand in 1969. The other studies suggest that the latter figure may be as high as forty thousand. The migration appears to have been a response to the tight labor markets in the middle sixties. Respondents report this to be the case, and the data shows the immigration to have peaked in these years.[5] The firms identified as significant employers of Puerto Ricans all had large numbers of relatively unattractive jobs, conforming to the description of secondary work in the dual labor-market hypothesis. A number of the employers described their own plants as "sweat shops," and the workers certainly thought of them in this way.

In the early sixties, jobs in these shops appear to have been held by older immigrants and native workers, especially blacks. In the middle sixties, these workers reportedly became a good deal more difficult to manage. Clashes between employees and supervisors and among the employees themselves became more frequent. Employers also seemed to feel that it became more difficult to recruit and retain native workers. However, employers ranked recruitment and turnover problems as secondary to that of the intractability of workers on the job. Faced with these difficulties, employers turned increasingly to the Puerto Rican labor force.

Puerto Ricans may have replaced individuals from a variety of different backgrounds, but employers placed particular emphasis on the severity of labor problems among black workers, and the single group of workers most frequently replaced by Puerto Ricans were

[4] Adriana Gianturco and Norman Aronin, *Boston's Spanish-Speaking Community* (Boston, Mass.: Action for Boston Community Development, October 1971); and Charles M. Sullivan, ed., *Five Ethnic Groups in Boston* (Boston, Mass.: Action for Boston Community Development and United Community Services of Metropolitan Boston, June 1972).

[5] Gianturco and Aronin, op. cit., pp. 8 and 16; Sullivan, op. cit., p. 35.

blacks. One employer reported that his neighbor's black foreman found it so difficult to manage black workers that he had decided one day never to hire another black and since then had been hiring Puerto Ricans instead. This story was consistent with the ethnic and racial composition of all the shops visited.

Most of the employers with whom the researchers talked claimed to have recruited their own Puerto Rican work force from walk-ins. A few employers reported that faced with a labor shortage (by which they meant a group of walk-in applicants they did not think they could manage) they had contacted community groups and religious leaders in the Spanish-speaking community. Everyone interviewed— employers, community leaders, and migrants—knew of someone who had actively recruited employees on the island. Generally, this meant that they had hired a Puerto Rican worker on the mainland and paid his fare to his native village to recruit employees for the shop. Those few community leaders known to have institutional contacts with Puerto Ricans reported that they frequently received requests from employers to recruit labor there.

RURAL ORIGINS OF THE MIGRANT WORKERS

The Puerto Rican labor force in Boston is overwhelmingly rural in origin, recruited from the labor surplus of agricultural communities in the island's hills and along its coast. They are, in other words, peasants and conform in speech and attitude to a recognizable peasant-type in Puerto Rican culture, the *jibero*. There is no indication that these people have lived for any period of time in one of the major cities of the island or in a mainland city.[6] Most have little command of English, many are illiterate, and virtually all are poorly educated, even in Spanish.[7]

None of these characteristics—rural background, language, education—seems to constitute a barrier to employment. Employers were much more concerned about high turnover.[8] A number mentioned a tendency among Puerto Ricans to leave suddenly without notice and

---

[6] Most migrants with whom the researchers talked had considered, at least implicitly, moving to other cities on the East Coast where they had relatives; the reason given for rejecting these alternatives was consistently the fear that their children would become addicted to drugs.

[7] Sullivan, op. cit., p. 6; and Gianturco and Aronin, op. cit., pp. 32, 34, and 36.

[8] Sullivan, op. cit., p. 71; and Gianturco and Aronin, op. cit., p. 74.

reappear weeks or months later expecting the old job. In many cases this is clearly a cultural problem that derives from the workers' rural background and persists because of communicaton difficulties with the employer. Another common story involved the worker who left his job suddenly and sent his brother to take his place. The last characteristic of the Puerto Rican labor force reported by employers was a tendency to use welfare and unemployment insurance. Statistics on the incidence of welfare dependency among Puerto Ricans tends to confirm this.[9] Surprisingly, the employers interviewed treated this either matter-of-factly or with some sympathy. The extreme resentment against welfare common among comparable managerial personnel in higher-wage enterprises was not encountered in this study.

The situation pictured is one in which employers offering low wages found themselves faced with significant labor shortages. Their response was to seek new sources of labor. This was a general pattern and in the communities surrounding Boston took the form of reviving traditional migration streams from French-speaking Canada, Portugal's Cape Verde, and, to a lesser extent, Greece, Italy, and Ireland. In Boston as well as in the surrounding communities, this phenomenon also led to the development of a new wave of immigration from Puerto Rico.

Conditions in Puerto Rico were ripe for emigration, but it is clear that active recruiting on the part of Boston employers provided a definite impetus. Since no employers admitted to doing any recruiting themselves, it is difficult to specify the recruitment pattern. But given the high turnover among Puerto Rican workers, it might be speculated that active recruiting was the work of large employers and that the smaller ones drew the fall-off from the migration streams stimulated by their larger neighbors. On the other hand, the cost of recruitment is low (round-trip fare to Puerto Rico is less than two hundred dollars), and even the smallest employer was probably not above sending a worker on a quick trip home at the peak of the production cycle.

Why Puerto Rico? Perhaps because it is the last large reserve of surplus labor among American citizens who can travel freely to the Boston area. One can, however, think of close substitutes in the black South, Appalachia, and the Southwest. A significant part of the phenomenon, therefore, appears to be the larger stream of the Puerto Rican agricultural migration. Since World War II, large numbers of Puerto Rican workers have come to work each year on New England farms under contracts negotiated and policed by the Puerto

---

[9] One study, for example, reports 49 percent of the household units receiving welfare payments.

Rican government. There is now a significant stream of noncontract migrant labor as well. It is probably this agricultural migration that alerted manufacturers to the readily available Puerto Rican labor pool. The agricultural migration did not produce permanent settlements of Puerto Ricans. After thirty years of annual migration, small colonies of Puerto Ricans are just beginning to appear in rural areas where they have been employed. The sudden growth of the Spanish-speaking community in Boston did not appear to be related to this.

JOB AND WORKER CHARACTERISTICS

If the Puerto Rican migration was initiated by employers in response to the increasing intractability of the black labor force, one wants to know why the black labor force suddenly became intractable and why the Puerto Ricans found the jobs acceptable. The answer lies in a closer analysis of the characteristics of the jobs and of the Puerto Ricans as employees.

As noted earlier, the jobs Puerto Ricans held tended to have the characteristics ascribed to secondary work in the dual labor-market hypothesis. Lacking opportunity for upward mobility, they offered little chance of advancement, training, or institutional connections.

The reasons for this limited mobility were varied. Generally, the job structure of the enterprise itself offered few avenues for promotion. In manufacturing, this appeared attributable to technology. Two patterns prevailed. In one, typified by a packaging firm, there was an overwhelming preponderance of unskilled jobs with few higher-level positions of any kind. The second pattern consisted of an essentially bimodal job structure with significant numbers of both unskilled and skilled jobs but few intermediate positions through which one could progress. The unskilled jobs, moreover, were often physically isolated from the others in the plant, so there was little opportunity for learning and limited information about what kind of openings in higher-level positions might be available. Shoe plants typically had this second type of job structure. In service industries, particularly hospitals, the lack of upward mobility seemed to be less a feature of the technology than of the institutional barriers created by professionalization.

Aside from technology, the major factor curtailing mobility or, perhaps more accurately, leading the labor force to perceive the jobs as lacking mobility, was that the industries were declining in the area and offered little prospect for life-time employment. A last factor involved in the lack of upward mobility was the seasonal and cyclical nature of the demand for labor. In several plants, these fluctuations were so frequent and so severe that the jobs offered no continuity of employment in which a series of skills could be accumulated. On the whole, however, this pattern was less pronounced than the researchers had expected.

The one other job characteristic that related interestingly to earlier studies of the dual labor market was the number of jobs in manufacturing that were unionized—well over half the sample.[10] Unionization, it is to be noted, seemed to have little effect on job characteristics. What appeared significant was that either the plant had a bimodal job structure itself or was part of an industry that did. The heart of the union organization and the focus of its influence on job characteristics was the skilled job. Unskilled jobs were organized as a by-product. For example, unskilled workers lacked real access to the formal grievance procedure, forcing them to resolve their problems personally with their foreman.

Union organization did exert some influence in wages. Several managers mentioned the difficulty of raising wages in the face of a shortage of unskilled workers because of the subsequent effect on the skilled wage. It might be argued that this deterred them from reacting to market scarcities through competition and increased their reliance on recruitment of new immigrant groups. This proposition, however, is dubious. The perceived labor shortage was one that could have been overcome only through a major change in the relative wages of unskilled workers, a change that would have driven the companies out of business.

ATTACHMENT TO THE ISLAND

The Puerto Rican labor force may be characterized in several different ways. Its most outstanding characteristics appear to be its extreme mobility, its underlying attachment to the island, and the temporary nature of its commitment to Boston. Discussions with community leaders and with the migrants themselves suggest that this is a population that continues in some fundamental sense to be rooted in its place of origin.[11] Typically, Puerto Ricans do not come to

---

[10] This seems to be confirmed by one of the sample surveys, which reports that 43 percent of the Puerto Ricans were union members. Sullivan, op. cit., p. 69.

[11] The survey data also suggests this. A sample in which one-fourth of the respondents were Cubans with no opportunity to return home showed that 22 percent planned to stay six months or less and that an additional 35

Boston to make a permanent life in the city. Rather they come planning to accumulate money and return to the island with funds to buy a farm or open a small business. Most are unable to realize this ambition, but they nonetheless return to deal with family problems, to visit, and to find temporary respite from income-earning activities. They may or may not return to Boston subsequently. Those who ultimately do settle and bring or form a family there reportedly do so only after several trips back and forth to the island. And often then they settle in Boston only by default after postponing the decision to return to the island rather than making a conscious decision to remain.

This pattern of mobility back and forth between Puerto Rico and the mainland also appears in the survey data, where it is muted by underreporting among the more mobile segment of the population.[12] The pattern is similar to that among blacks in the rural South in the early 1960s. Practically everyone had been North at one time or another, and there was a constant flux of people returning home temporarily and departing again to visit or live with some relative in the North.

This suggests that the conventional view of migration as a single move between two points missed the essence of the process. It creates the impression that what is occurring is the accumulation of a stock of people in Boston and a reduction in the stock of people in Puerto Rico. In fact, the migration process is characterized more accurately as a continual flow of people originating on the island, passing through Boston, and moving back to Puerto Rico. The numbers of Puerto Ricans in Boston, this suggests, may be constant, but the individuals are not. Out of this flow, of course, a group is eventually formed with a more permanent attachment to the city, but at the early stage of the migratory process, on which this study focused, this number is a relatively small portion of the labor force.

The attachment of the migrants to Puerto Rico relates to the second reason why they found the secondary jobs in the Boston labor market acceptable. From the perspective of the island—particularly the parts of the island where the migrants originate—such work lies close to the top of the hierarchy. Puerto Rico has undergone extremely

---

percent had no definite plans about length of stay. Gianturco and Aronin, op. cit., p. 11.

[12] Ibid., pp. 15 and 16. Half the sample, 25 percent of which was Cuban, had returned home at least once since moving to the United States, and 16 percent returned home three or more times. Mobility within Boston is also high: over half the sample had lived three or more places in Boston.

rapid development in the last twenty years. Its effect has been a shift in the economic structure from dependence on sugar cane and coffee to manufacturing and services. The type of manufacturing and services on which this transition has hinged involves light assembly work, considerable warehousing, and garment and shoe production essentially comparable to that offered in Boston and in some cases exactly the same. The driving force in the growth of the service sector has been tourism so that, again, the types of jobs associated with local economic development are not unlike the restaurant, hotel, and hospital jobs offered in Boston.

Little of this development, however, has occurred in the regions of the island from which the migrants come. Employment there continues to be confined to agricultural labor. The work is associated with an earlier period in Puerto Rican history; it is also, by any objective standard, extremely demanding, physically debilitating, and unpleasant. The younger generation has refused to do it. As a result, in the last five years, as the older generation has died or retired, these traditional industries have faced such a severe labor shortage that they have been forced to adopt a radical program of mechanization and technological change. Shortages are so severe, in fact, that the government has heavily subsidized the agricultural wage rate. But it is the contrast between these traditional jobs and those of the Boston labor market that seems to make the latter acceptable to the migrants. The continual backflow of migrants to the island preserves and reinforces that perspective.

EARLIER BLACK MIGRANTS

There is an hypothesis about why the native workers find the jobs in Boston unacceptable, and this hypothesis is congruent with the explanation of why the Puerto Rican workers do not. Native black workers are the children of an earlier generation of migrants who left the South in the 1940s and 1950s. Their migratory process from the black communities of the rural South to the Northern ghettos is similar to that of the Puerto Ricans: a continual stream of people moving through the Northern cities and back to the South again, leaving a relatively permanent population in the North, who raise families there.

For the first generation of migrants, whose perspective is that of the rural South, the secondary jobs are attractive, resulting in the initial concentration of blacks in these jobs. Their children, however, raised in the North with a Northern perspective, see these jobs as the bottom of the social hierarchy and find them unacceptable, just as the Puerto Rican migrants (and probably the migrant parents of black youths as well) find agricultural work unacceptable. This explanation of the growing intransigence of the black labor force in the mid-1960s describes, therefore, a shift in the composition of the black labor force from one dominated by first-generation immigrants to one dominated by the second generation.

Of course, the behavior of the labor force is a function of several variables including job attitudes and economic conditions and opportunities. The generally depressed economic conditions in the late 1950s and early 1960s masked the change in the composition of the labor force, whereas the manifestations of that change in the mid-1960s were heightened by the extremely tight labor markets, the civil rights movement, and the increased accessibility of the welfare system.

The preceding discussion has concentrated exclusively on the black population, although secondary jobs, both before and after the entrance of Puerto Ricans, were held by a number of other immigrant groups as well. This emphasis corresponds to employer comments that suggest the displacement was basically one of blacks by Puerto Ricans. The presence of other immigrant groups is nonetheless consistent with the preceding hypothesis: there were no second-generation workers and the immigrant labor force consisted either of recent arrivals or older people from some earlier migratory wave. The absence of recent black migrants is difficult to explain. Perhaps migration from the South has stopped, or perhaps employers do not distinguish between Northern and Southern blacks. Discrimination based solely on race at any rate is ruled out by the presence of Spanish-speaking and Haitian blacks.

The major alternatives to the preceding explanation and the one most consistent with current economic theory rely on the differences in the information about jobs available to the various groups in the labor force and on differences in the education and training available to each group. It was exceedingly difficult to evaluate these alternatives in the context of the case study. Both were completely inappropriate to the spirit and language of the interviews, and both were foreign to the participants in the labor market studied: employers, workers, community leaders, and employees in other labor market situations.

If information or training is important, it is clearly operated at a level once removed from the consciousness of the market practitioners. Employers generally did not mention language deficiencies until asked; and discussions of the communication problem suggested that as long as there was someone around who spoke both languages, however imperfectly, this problem could be overcome. In several shops, there was more than one non-English-speaking language group. The low level of educational attainment among the Puerto Ricans was generally not mentioned, and many employers were unaware of it.

Similarly, there was no obvious difference in the amount of job information available to the different groups of workers. The active role of employers in disseminating the information that developed this new source of labor has already been noted. Comments from each of the different types of respondents suggested the effectiveness of the network of friends and relatives in spreading job information. Employers' comments, particularly, emphasized the speed with which it operated: once a Puerto Rican was hired, as many additional workers as were necessary could be recruited through him.

GENERAL IMPLICATIONS

Three key elements are present in the preceding study: a set of dead-end jobs unacceptable to the native labor force; a new migrant population whose labor-market perspective was molded in an under-developed region in which comparable jobs are acceptable; and a second generation who are descended from an earlier migrant stream that was originally recruited to fill the jobs and who have adopted the labor-market perspective of the natives. It is the flow-like character of the Puerto Rican migration that makes the jobs acceptable: the temporary nature of their stays renders them indifferent to the lack of security and advancement, and the periodic visits to Puerto Rico reinforce the perspective of the island labor market, which vests the jobs with a much higher relative status than they have among native workers. The flow also affects the size of the labor force, making it highly responsive to variations in economic conditions. The second generation, who represent a fall-out from a similar flow, are distinguished from their progenitors by their permanent attachment to the new area. This attachment renders the group's size unresponsive to economic conditions and fosters tension between opportunities and aspirations.

The history of industrial societies suggests that these traits may not be peculiar to the Puerto Rican migration, but rather a common occurrence in the process of economic development. Industrial economies may tend to generate a series of unstable, dead-end jobs that the native labor force, except in periods of dire unemployment, will reject, forcing employers to recruit migrants from underdeveloped regions, at home or abroad. These migrants may in turn produce a second generation, who reject their parents' jobs, generating conflicts over upward mobility within the developed region and forcing employers to look farther afield for new migrants to fill the bottom positions in the economy. There is a corresponding trend in the underdeveloped region when the migrant stream returns home with an accumulation of capital, skill, and aspirations acquired in the developed region. Such a returning population is a key factor in engendering economic development in backward regions and spreading industrialization.[13] As it progresses, the developing region not only becomes increasingly less useful as a supply of labor, but eventually must add its own demands for unspoiled labor to that of other industrial nations.

One of the chief differences between the United States and the European economies is the role played by foreign immigration as opposed to the migration of native workers from underdeveloped regions within national boundaries. European development depended initially on internal migration. A result is that the distinction between recent migrants and native workers was less obvious and, in particular, upward mobility was easier for second generation workers. As internal sources of labor were exhausted, however, European countries were forced to rely increasingly on foreign immigrants.

This reliance has become painfully obvious in recent years with the massive influx of Italians, Turks, and Eastern Europeans to Germany and Switzerland; the so-called colored migration to England; and the flow of Spanish, Portuguese, and North African workers to France. Actually, the use of foreign labor in Europe can be traced back to the early part of this century.[14] The role of migrants in the economy and the tensions associated with them are similar to those suggested by the study of the Puerto Rican migration to Boston. In American economic development the European process was reversed.

---

[13] See Bernard Kayser, *Manpower Movements & Labour Markets* (Paris: Organization for European Cooperation and Development, 1971), pp. 93–152. For Puerto Rico in particular, *see* Jose Hernandez Alvarez, *Return Migration to Puerto Rico,* Population Monograph Series No. 1 (Berkeley, Calif.: Institute of International Studies, University of California, 1967).

[14] Charles P. Kindleberger, *Europe's Postwar Growth: The Role of Labor Supply* (Cambridge, Mass: Harvard University Press, 1967).

Initial reliance was on foreign immigrants.[15] It was only later, that American industry turned to domestic areas of underdevelopment.

THE SOUTH'S CASTE SOLUTION

This view of the process suggests that the racial tensions experienced in the United States in the 1960s were rooted in the curtailment of open foreign immigration in 1923. Eliminating the traditional sources of new workers for secondary jobs forced employers to turn from underdeveloped foreign areas to backward regions within their own borders. The full effect of this was delayed by the depression of the 1930s, but in the 1940s and 1950s it resulted in large-scale black migration to the Northern cities. The migrants were recruited for, and largely confined to, secondary jobs because these jobs were an improvement over the opportunities available in the South. Because their residence in the North was often viewed as temporary, they were accepted passively. By the late 1950s, however, a second generation of black workers, who had grown up in the North, was entering the labor force. They did not view the available jobs from the perspective of the rural South and so found them unacceptable. The pressure of this second generation for upward mobility and the resistance of the groups commanding the jobs the younger blacks were seeking were the forces basically responsible for the clashes of that era.

Seen in this way, the problem of the blacks is thus essentially a problem of immigrant groups, and a rereading of earlier American history shows that similar clashes between natives or earlier ethnic migrants and the children of more recent immigrants occurred frequently in the latter half of the nineteenth century and the early part of the twentieth.

Two factors, however, make the black case different. First—though less important, because the newer migrants were distinguished by

[15] Although it seems a little far-fetched to equate the role of earlier immigrants with that of the Puerto Ricans and blacks in a hypothesis which depends so heavily upon the flow-like character of the migration process, the data turns out to be surprisingly supportive of this view. *See* Simon Kuznets and Ernest Rubin, *Immigration and the Foreign Born*, Occasional Paper No. 46, Part II (New York: National Bureau of Economic Research, 1954), pp. 26–30 and 39.

race—it was impossible to obscure, let alone moderate the black migrants' separate identity, and this undoubtedly made the barriers to upward mobility a good deal more rigid. Second, these black migrants from the South came from a region that appeared to have found, in the racial caste system, an alternative to migration as a means of filling the jobs in the secondary sector. The social and legal structure of the South impressed on blacks the fact that their role was to occupy lower stations in the job structure, however menial and unattractive. In terms of social stability, this solution is more attractive than that of migration because it precludes the rise of an intractable second generation that might threaten the jobs of more established groups.

With the enactment of severe limitations on foreign immigration and the resultant decline in the number of new migrants, the Southern solution was bound to appeal to Northern employers as well. Thus, it can be argued that the blacks had to fight especially hard to insure the upward mobility and resist any Northern attempt to impose the Southern caste solution. Certainly, this is how the black leadership perceived the problem. The central issue of the 1960s may then be interpreted as whether the country would resolve the secondary labor market through the racial caste system of the South or seek an alternative compatible with the liberal ideology of the North and with the basic national documents.

Although it remains unclear whether the liberal alternative will be realized, the rhetoric of the civil rights movement, the Black Power movement, and the concomitant changes in black consciousness have effectively destroyed the sociological foundations of the caste system that prevailed in the South. Consequently, the problems of the second generation of blacks in the North cannot be resolved in the Southern way. And if this is true, then, in addition to whatever racial questions remain to be resolved in the North, there also remains the problem of the secondary labor market.

One obvious response to the problems immigration poses for the economy is to curtail the number of jobs that immigrants are recruited to fill. The Boston study suggests a certain caution about a policy of curtailing migration through the elimination of secondary jobs. A number of these jobs, it was noted, are complements to skilled work in the primary sector, and the cost of finding other means of accomplishing such work might be considerable. The argument has been put forth elsewhere that many such jobs are complementary in another sense not directly observable in a study of this kind: they are generated to stabilize employment opportunities in other parts of the economic system.[16]

Of perhaps equal import is a characteristic of the Boston jobs not emphasized earlier. The secondary sector in the Boston area is closely related to conditions motivating the export of jobs to under-developed countries. In a number of industries—particularly the man-ufacture of shoes, textiles, and garments—employers saw the use of immigrants as an alternative to relocation abroad.

ORGANIZATION OF THE MIGRANT STREAM

If the secondary sector is to be maintained and immigration remains a major source of labor, the policies affecting the organization of the migration stream must be explored. Slowing the development of a second generation—and, consequently, reducing the problems created by the desire for upward mobility—should prove more feasible in the future. The migration stream will once again be dominated by for-eigners, the forms and conditions of whose work are governed by visa. In the last thirty years migration has primarily involved Ameri-can citizens whose freedom of movement is protected by constitutional guarantees.

The two polar forms taken by the migrant stream are both illus-trated by the Puerto Rican migration to New England. One pole is the industrial form in which movement is completely unrestricted. The migrants settle in a community and change their jobs and places of residence more or less at will. The opposite pole may be seen among agricultural workers: generally under contract to a specific employer, these migrants live on the farm in housing the employer provides; they are isolated from the local community and, upon the expiration of the contract, return directly to the island, without other stopovers on the continent. Between these two polar extremes are a variety of possible intermediate forms in which the opportunities for the migrant to develop other social and economic contacts at the destination are greater than those of contract agricultural workers but more circumscribed than in the case of the industrial migrant.

---

[16] Michael J. Piore, *Upward Mobility, Job Monotony, and Labor Market Structure,* Massachusetts Institute of Technology Economics Working Paper No. 90 (Cambridge, Mass.: MIT Department of Economics, September 1972).

Few of these intermediate positions are realized in the case of the Puerto Rican migration.

In general, it appears that the development of a second generation occurs more rapidly in the more open migration process with the migrant free to pick his employer, his place of residence, and his date of return. Thus Puerto Rican industrial migrants have developed a second generation much more rapidly than have the agricultural migrants. It should be noted, however, that some "fallout" of permanent residents has occurred even among agricultural workers, and, after twenty years of migration, tiny communities of Puerto Ricans were scattered throughout rural New England. These were one-time agricultural migrants who decided to remain for the winter and were joined by their families.

The existence of these communities has reduced the agricultural migrants' isolation and their dependence on their employers. This has reportedly reduced the tractability of the agricultural workers. That such a fallout eventually occurred does not detract, however, from the basic points that the rate of fallout is clearly a function of the way in which the migration process occurs and that there are forms of migration which retard that process and prolong the period a given migrant source will serve its industrial function.

A related point is that the range of feasible forms the migration might take is probably not independent of the functions that the migrants are drawn to perform. Agriculture, because of the geographic isolation involved, lends itself to a contained migration process in a way that industry does not. That so many Puerto Rican migrants are recruited by service and small industrial concerns makes it unlikely that the rate of permanent settlement can be controlled.

UNAVOIDABLE SECOND GENERATION

Further specific points about the organization of migration can now be put forth. First, the rate at which second generation develops clearly depends on whether or not the migrants are permitted to bring their families; and it appears that the fallout might be completely blocked by limiting migration to men. It must be noted, however, that a number of jobs for which migrants are recruited employ men and women interchangeably and some, such as domestic service, use females almost exclusively. To the extent that there are jobs available for women, it may be difficult to prevent the migration from developing a second generation.

Second, it is difficult to impose a particular organizational form through legal requirements. The process of migration described here is one having both a strong employer demand for labor and a strong desire among the migrants for work. Moreover, a number of the characteristics generating the demand for migrants—the desire of the native labor force to escape the effects of unpredictable fluctuations in the demand for industrial output and the employer's need to respond to such fluctuations—are not conducive to forms of organization that are apt to slow the development of a second generation.

Under these circumstances, efforts to prevent a second generation from forming would foster an illegal market. Indeed, such an illegal market is already present in Boston in the form of a large group of illegal migrants from Latin America who live under the umbrella of the Puerto Rican and Cuban populations. Employers report that illegal migrants form a stable work force, and this very stability may be conducive to the development of a second generation labor force. This labor force will have the protection of American citizenship, and this alone would be enough to create a strong contrast between their behavior and that of their parents. Such a second generation will resent the treatment of their parents, whose illegal status opens them to exploitation by employers threatening to report them to authorities.

It seems doubtful, then, that society can avoid the problems of the second generation through controlling the migrant stream. If, as appears to be the case, the economy cannot operate without a migrant stream that produces a second generation, then the only alternative for public policy is to focus on opening the channels of upward mobility.

Ethnicity and Health Delivery Systems

LEONA GROSSMAN

Leona Grossman, MSW and MPH, is Director, Department of Social Work, Michael Reese Hospital and Medical Center, and Lecturer at the School of Social Service Administration, the University of Chicago, Chicago, Illinois.

EDITORS' COMMENT

The following three essays discuss particular policy recommendations based on an understanding and analysis of the needs of the individual in a pluralistic society. The use of social services by ethnic groups reflects the cultural backgrounds of those groups. Grossman points out how the differential use of medical care among ethnic groups is linked to their own particular experiences of life. Different ethnic populations perceive symptoms differently, and the decision to seek medical care is often related to two factors: (1) the prevalence and familiarity of the symptom, and (2) the degree to which the symptom prevents functioning in accustomed roles. This paper examines the responses of selected ethnic groups to symptoms and discusses their use of medical facilities. Suggestions are made for changes in the medical care system in the light of each ethnic group's response. The recommendations suggest that similar adaptations of other service delivery systems will result in a more effective implementation of social welfare policies.

———————

The observation has repeatedly been made that ethnic populations tend to underutilize or misutilize hospital facilities. Ethnics are said to rely on emergency room care instead of keeping regular clinic appointments or to prefer locally based health practitioners to community hospitals.[1] Research on the utilization of hospital services led Berkanovic and Reeder to identify three factors in explanation of this phenomenon: "(1) unequal access, (2) culture of poverty, and (3) cultural and social psychological differences usually related to ethnicity and socioeconomic status."[2]

Each one of these explanations has some validity. Certainly, the socioeconomic factors suggested by the phrase "unequal access" are important. However, studies from the United Kingdom, where there is National Health Care, indicate that class differentials affect utilization even though the service is free. This could suggest that people in the lower socioeconomic classes participate in a "culture of poverty" and need to "learn the skills essential for participation in the 'mainstream.'" They need to be "taught how to use the system." This is arguable. The third factor, which has immediate relevance to this paper, suggests that utilization of medical care is "linked to differential experiences of life."[3]

DIFFERING PERCEPTIONS OF ILLNESS

Different ethnic populations perceive systems of illness differently. The prevalence of a symptom or disease and the individual's famil-

---

[1] J. B. McKinlay, "Some Approaches and Problems in the Study of the Use of Services—An Overview," *Journal of Health and Social Behavior*, 3 (April 1972), pp. 115–151.

[2] Emil Berkanovic and Leo G. Reeder, "Ethnic, Economic, and Social Psychological Factors in the Source of Medical Care," *Social Problems*, 21 (Fall 1973), p. 248.

[3] Ibid, pp. 250–251.

iarity with it tend to influence the decision to seek or forego medical care. The degree to which a symptom prevents the person from carrying out accustomed roles is another factor in this decision.

Although ethnic populations tend to define different diseases as common or serious, a variety of factors, as Allard points out, are likely to influence the response to the disease:

> The severity of the symptoms which will be endured, however, depends on such cultural factors as definitions of illness and such physiological factors as pain threshold, as well as upon ecological conditions such as overall disease incidence, frequency of illness in the community and the types of disease prevalent.[4]

In most ethnic populations, mild or common symptoms are handled by parents, relatives, and friends. This is often referred to as the "lay diagnostic network." [5] Only when symptoms become severe and incapacitating is professional advice sought.

Depending on how the symptom is defined, an initial decision is made to go to a local physician/folk curer or to the emergency room or outpatient department of a hospital. If the individual believes his symptoms are related to his breaking of a taboo or to some supernatural factor, the specialist chosen will be expected to address himself to these social causes. Most folk systems of medical care treat diseases both socially and medically, although they are more likely to concentrate on individual symptoms and not be concerned with the complexity of disease syndromes and involved diagnostic procedures.

Zola and his associates developed matching samples of Irish and Italian outpatient populations attending eye, ear, nose, and throat clinics in two large Boston hospitals.[6] Their findings indicated that these two populations exercised a selective process in the symptoms they brought to the physician. There were also differences in responses to similar diseases. The Irish tended to locate their chief complaints in specific organs (the ear, eye, nose, and throat) and indicated that these organs aroused the greatest anxiety in them. The Italians, even

[4] Alexander Allard, Jr., *Adaptation in Cultural Evolution: An Approach to Medical Anthropology* (New York: Columbia University Press, 1970), p. 114.

[5] Eliot Freidson, *Patient's Views of Medical Practice* (New York: Russell Sage Foundation, 1970).

[6] Irving Kenneth Zola, "Culture and Symptoms—An Analysis of Patients' Presenting Complaints," *American Sociological Review*, 31 (October 1966), pp. 615–630.

though they were suffering from the same diseases, tended not to localize their complaints or concerns on those organs. The level of dysfunction caused by the illness varied: the Irish tended to limit their dysfunction to the organs affected; the Italians generalized their difficulties to all parts of their bodies and noted more bodily dysfunction. The Irish also tended to deny pain more often than the Italians.

Zola explains these ethnic differences in terms of the "fit" between certain bodily states and dominant value orientations.[7] Ethnic groups with varying world views use different defensive maneuvers to perceive and handle stress. The Italians, he noted, handle stress through overreaction or "overdramatization," and the Irish tend to use denial and displacement—into alcoholism or fantasy. Furthermore, Zola believes that ideologies of sin and guilt pervade Irish culture.

> Perhaps their three most favored locations of symptoms (the eyes, ears, and throat) might be understood as symbolic reflections of the more immediate source of their sin and guilt—what they should not have seen; what they should not have heard; and what they should not have said.[8]

Zola admitted many possible loopholes in his conclusions, but his ultimate aim was to induce medical practitioners to include ethnic differentials in their diagnoses and to bring them to recognize that, in adhering only to rational scientific approaches, much can be overlooked. He tried to

> . . . present evidence showing that the very labelling and definition of a bodily state as a symptom or as a problem is, in itself, a part of a social process . . . ignoring what constitutes a deviation in the eyes of the individual and his society may obscure important aspects of our understanding and eventually our philosophies of treatment and control of illness.[9]

One of the key concepts in understanding behaviors in illness is that of social perception.

EXPERIENCE OF PAIN

A prime motivator in seeking medical care is the experience of pain. Pain as a symptom has been investigated physiologically and pharmacologically, but only a few researchers have looked into the ethnocultural features of pain responses. Zborowski, a notable exception,

[7] Ibid., p. 626.
[8] Ibid., p. 628.
[9] Ibid., p. 620.

conducted a three-year study in which he contrasted the responses to pain among Jews, Italians, Irish, and old Americans.[10] His basic assumption was that physiological needs are learned and intricately bound to cultural values. Thus, cultural groups develop characteristic response patterns to physiological stimuli as well as characteristic attitudes toward pain. To Zborowski, pain responses are communications. Using Kluckhohn's schema of cultural orientations to time, he concluded that groups who are "future-oriented" might evaluate pain in terms of the consequences on life to come, rather than in terms of the immediate severity of the pain and the satisfaction with receiving relief from it.[11] Future-oriented Jews represent the former and tend to suffer anxiety about future adequacy when pain occurs. Italians tend to be present-oriented and to want relief.

Zborowski's study also showed how the different groups acted in responding to pain. Old Americans, who tended to be conditioned by repressive patterns of family interaction, did not believe that complaining would bring any results and therefore were contained in their responses. The Irish also played down pain and diagnoses. They were likely to speak of "suffering" rather than "pain" and to regard pain as something private, which was not to be described to others. Pain was regarded as a test of manhood, not a symptom.

Both Jews and Italians were strongly accustomed to sympathetic feedback from their family groups and tended to dramatize their pain. Italians in Zborowski's study regarded pain as something social, something to be shared. They saw the relief of pain as more important than its etiology, which may be the reason pain relievers are said to have a rapid effect on Italian patients. The Jew, in contrast to the Italian, tended to combine his tendency toward dramatization with a strong interest in the etiology of his affliction. Jews, as Novak noted, "will know symptoms, diseases, drugs, and remedies with a precision and detail unmatched by other ethnic groups. Pain is the drama of the self in history, and the Jew loves to enliven it." [12]

Zborowski also noted different reactions toward doctors among patients experiencing pain. The old Americans and Irish expressed

[10] Mark Zborowski, "Cultural Components in Responses to Pain," *Journal of Social Issues*, 8 (1952), pp. 16–30. *See also* Zborowski, *People in Pain* (San Francisco: Jossey-Bass, 1969).

[11] Florence R. Kluckhohn, "Dominant and Substitute Profiles of Cultural Orientation," *Social Forces*, 28 (1950), p. 350 ff.

[12] Michael Novak, *The Rise of the Unmeltable Ethnics* (New York: Macmillan Co., 1973), p. 28.

confidence in the doctors' skills, accepted their patient roles, and expressed satisfaction in the care they were getting. The Italians were more critical and demanding, the Jews decidedly more skeptical. The Irish and Jews both showed heightened anxieties about their bodies and tended more toward hypochondria. The old Americans tended to attribute illness to external factors. The Irish blamed themselves. One of Zborowski's interesting conclusions was that similar patterns of reactions to pain need not necessarily have the same function in different cultures.

ILLNESS BEHAVIOR

Suchman carries the analyses into another sphere. He starts with the hypothesis that differences among ethnic groups in behavior during illness and in patterns of seeking medical care are "associated with variations in the form of social organization of the ethnic groups." [13] The original data for his analyses were collected in the Washington Heights section of New York City between November 1960 and April 1961. The six major ethnic and religious categories he used were Negro, Puerto Rican, Jewish, Protestant, Catholic, and Irish-born Catholic.

His analysis led to the conclusion that when an ethnic group maintained strong ties among its members, there was a decrease in the need for "a cognitive understanding of disease." Members of a close-knit group expressed greater skepticism of outside professional medical help and were more inclined to seek aid within their group. Significant correlations were also found between traditionalism in family organization and resistance to accepting the "sick role": "Strong family authority acts against giving in to illness." This was particularly noted among the Irish, Puerto Ricans, and Negroes. Suchman concludes that the more "parochial," that is, the more traditional or closed a group tends to be, the more difficulty it will have in accepting modern medical care. For more "cosmopolitan" groups, ones that are more open and that encourage their members to be individualistic, accepting modern medical care is easier.

Suchman's subsequent articles supported his original hypothesis, correlating parochialism and cosmopolitanism in social structures

[13] Edward A. Suchman, "Sociomedical Variations Among Ethnic Groups," *American Journal of Sociology*, 52 (November 1964), pp. 319–331.

with adjustment to modern medical care systems.[14] He traced the influence of these cultural orientations through five stages of illness: symptom experience, assumption of sick role, medical care contract, dependent-patient role, and recovery or rehabilitation. In each stage he isolated component elements and found that they upheld his theory. He pointed out that these findings suggested the need for "two disparate approaches by the medical profession" and added that ". . . it is essential that the medical program become a part of the popular health culture of the group." [15]

In 1970, Suchman's hypotheses, which had been dominating medical sociology and health planning, were retested in Los Angeles by Reeder and Berkanovic.[16] Their sample was different from Suchman's. It contained 15 percent Mexican-Americans (largely native-born Americans), 25 percent blacks, 9 percent Puerto Ricans, 6 percent Jews, and 45 percent Protestants. The Los Angeles sample also had twice as many English-speaking persons. These investigators concluded that the relationships among demographic, structural, ethnic, and medical orientations were more complex than Suchman had originally found and their evidence often contradicted Suchman's conclusions about the influence of cosmopolitanism and parochialism.

Reeder and Berkanovic offered some possible explanations for the variance. They felt the time lapse had an effect. Between 1960 and 1970 the general rise in consumerism had been especially strong in the health care field. Ethnic revivals and community action programs had also led to local efforts for control of health services. This fact may account for the Los Angeles study's high correlation between parochialism and modern medical orientations. In Suchman's original study the members of parochial groups had been the least informed segments of the community about contemporary medicine and had been less oriented toward the use of modern medical care than other groups. However, the parochials in the later study were knowledgeable and "by virtue of living in ethnically exclusive enclaves, . . . the least skeptical about the medical care available to them." It seemed that

[14] Edward A. Suchman, "Social Patterns of Illness and Medical Care," *Journal of Health and Human Behavior,* 6 (Spring 1965), pp. 2–16; and "Health Orientation and Medical Care," *American Journal of Public Health,* 56 (January 1966), pp. 98–105.

[15] Suchman, "Health Orientation and Medical Care," p. 104.

[16] Leo G. Reeder and Emil Berkanovic, "Sociological Concomitants of Health Orientations: A Partial Replication of Suchman," *Journal of Health and Social Behavior,* 14 (June 1973), pp. 134–143.

the more ethnic groups were directly involved with the medical systems available to them, the more they tended to accept them.

These studies are just a few of those that make it clear that illness behavior affects the way services are used. Ethnic patterns affect how people of differing ethnic commitments respond to a range of symptoms, what they expect in treatment, and how they assume the sick role.

Parsons's classic model of the sick role, which was originally published in 1951 and which has long dominated sociological thinking, reduces the rich potentiality of cultural diversity to a one-dimensional frame of reference.[17] His model assumes that American society has an homogenized social structure, an assumption that reflects the assimilationist, melting-pot orientations typical of the era in which Parsons developed his theory. Instead of noting the many kinds of culturally determined sick roles and the many ways of passing from illness to health, the Parsonian model represents only those forms of adaptation to illness sanctioned by middle-class white Protestant America. It assumes the ideal of a nuclear family structure. It postulates that illness is always motivated and characterizes it as a form of deviant behavior because it violates normative rules and institutionalized expectations. The model places an obligation on the ill person to accept the dependent role, to tell all, to let others care for his body, and to get over being sick. There is no allowance for solutions that may differ. This stereotypic pattern has dominated attitudes of professionals in medical care systems and has had a powerful influence on shaping American medical institutions.

ILLNESS AND CULTURE

It is illuminating to consider the orientations toward health and illness of some special populations in urban settings. Hispanic groups in the United States are currently considered to be the second largest ethnic population. Despite common language and shared heritage, however, Hispanics are not a homogeneous group. Differing levels of social integration, socioeconomic class, geographical origins, education, and occupation affect their beliefs and behaviors.

Earlier studies on Mexican-Americans in the Southwest were unfortunately generalized to Hispanic populations as a whole. Bearing this in mind, there is still evidence that a developed folk tradi-

[17] Talcott Parsons, "Definitions of Health and Illness in the Light of American Values and Social Structure," in Gartley Jaco, ed., *Patients, Physicians & Illness* (New York: Free Press, 1972), pp. 107–127.

tion in medicine persists where there are Hispanic communities. Despite the level of sophistication of some members of these groups, the folkways endure and are often found side by side with modern medical practices.

Studies indicate that Hispanics classify illnesses as natural ("good") or artificial ("bad" or "unnatural") diseases. The natural illnesses are related to "God's will" and fate, whereas artificial illnesses are due to evil practiced by people, such as witchcraft. These categories pertain to both physical and mental conditions.[18] When diseases are considered to be the result of witchcraft or magic, a folk healer (*curandero*) or a witch (*bruja*) is consulted, and the patient is subjected to a succession of magico-ritualistic procedures. There is a well-defined folk nomenclature of diagnostic conditions for which etiology and ritualistic treatment are specified. *Mal de susto* ("magical fright"), *empacho* ("swelling of abdomen"), *latido* ("palpitation"), *mal ojo* ("evil eye"), and *mollera caida* ("fallen fontanelle") are some such terms, which Clark and others have studied.[19]

Hispanics, Saunders pointed out, believe that health is a "matter of chance and . . . that there is very little a person can do to keep it." [20] Such fatalism is no less a characteristic of the Hispanic folk tradition than strong family solidarity, orientation to the present, male dominance, or personalism. The Hispanic culture treats supernatural forces as social realities, and such a belief system naturally cultivates a special variety of health-related syndromes and phenomena. Among them are *ataque* (seizures and attacks) and other altered states of consciousness. All this, along with various forms of spiritualism, *curanderismo,* and a rich pharmacopoeia, the products of which are displayed in the numerous neighborhood *botanicas,* constitutes a competing model of curing.

[18] Lyle Saunders, *Cultural Differences and Medical Care: The Case of the Spanish-speaking People of the Southwest* (New York: Russell Sage Foundation, 1954); L. Saunders and G. Himes, "Folk Medicine and Medical Practices," *Journal of Medical Education,* 28 (September 1953), pp. 43–46; Julian Sanora, Lyle Saunders, and Richard F. Larson, "Knowledge about Specific Diseases in Four Selected Samples," *Journal of Health and Human Behavior,* 3 (Fall 1962), pp. 176–185.

[19] Margaret Clark, *Health in the Mexican-American Culture* (Berkeley and Los Angeles: University of California Press, 1959); Arthur J. Rubel, *Across the Tracks: Mexican Americans in a Texas City* (Austin, Texas: University of Texas Press, 1966); and Rubel, "Concepts of Disease in Mexican-American Culture," *American Anthropologist,* 62 (October 1960), pp. 795–814.

[20] Saunders, op. cit.

Hispanic culture also maintains a long-established belief in the necessity of balances between hot and cold and wet and dry.[21] This is connected historically with the humoral theory of ancient Greek medicine. Urban living has not weakened the impact of these folk beliefs. A recent study of a Puerto Rican neighborhood in New York City revealed that there was a continuing commitment to the hot-cold theory by Puerto Ricans attending the local outpatient department of a large hospital.[22]

Puerto Ricans divide diseases, medicines, and foods into *frio* ("cold"), *fresco* ("cool"), and *caliente* ("hot"). For example, in infant feeding, the usual evaporated milk formula is considered hot and whole milk is cold. Should the infant develop a rash, which is considered hot, Puerto Rican mothers automatically switch to whole milk (cold), or else they introduce a "neutralizing" (cool) substance into the baby's diet, such as barley water, mannitol, or magnesium carbonate. These substances cause diarrhea. Physicians who treat Puerto Rican families should be aware of these practices so that such neutralizing substances do not create additional medical problems.

In many situations this system of the hot-cold balance has been found to be empirically sound; for example, the tradition prescribes bland or cold foods for ulcers, which are classified as hot. The classifications of the system vary with different groups, and the practices seem to be based more on individual experience than on organized logic. Professionals need to probe to discover the specific beliefs of the patients with whom they are working.

Hispanic tradition, then, considers illness as an "unbalance of intrapersonal elements between the individual and his socio-religious environment." [23] The curing process is a method by which the individual is helped to reintegrate into his group. The family and ethnic group play focal roles in the processes of diagnosis, treatment, and rehabilitation. Hospitalization is avoided whenever possible. It is generally believed that curing folk-defined illnesses has a two-fold purpose: (1) preserving and reintegrating Hispanic cultural beliefs, and (2) resolving tensions and conflicts within the group so as to restore equilibrium. The medical care system acts as a social control

---

[21] Richard L. Currier, "The Hot-Cold Syndrome and Symbolic Balance in Mexican and Spanish-American Folk Medicine," *Ethnology*, 5 (July 1966), pp. 251–263.

[22] Alan Harwood, "The Hot-Cold Theory of Disease," *Journal of the American Medical Association*, 216 (May 17, 1971), pp. 1153–1158.

[23] Elias Sevilla-Casas, "Studies on the Mental Health Situation of Mexican-Americans." Unpublished manuscript, Chicago, January 1973.

mechanism for insuring the perpetuation of the culture.

Another population of particular interest is the Amerindians, and specifically the Navaho. The Navaho nation is one of the largest of American Indian populations and perhaps one of the most distinctive. Although there have been numerous changes in Navaho traditions over the years, their basic orientation toward health and disease has persisted. Health is the reflection of an unseen harmony between man and his environment. It encompasses the natural world, fellow men, and the supernatural. Illness indicates an unbalance between man and his environment and is usually attributed to the breaking of a taboo, to contact with ghosts, or to malevolence on the part of others.

There is a close connection between curing and religious rituals. The "diviner" and the "singer" are essential to recovery. Even though the Navaho avails himself of many of the services of modern medicine, these traditions persist. The doctor can rid him of pain and germs, but he cannot help the Navaho achieve harmony with his environment. For example, a Navaho just discharged from the hospital is likely to be anxious to complete the religious part of his cure, and this is not accomplished until a *sing* has been held. A Navaho "singer" described it this way:

> As I see it, all the diseases which hurt the Navaho people may be divided into three kinds. There are those diseases that we medicine men have given up on. We know that you white doctors have better cures than we do. One of the diseases of that sort is tuberculosis. Then there is a sickness which comes from getting too close to where lightning has struck. Right now there are probably some patients in this hospital who are sick from that illness and you doctors have no way of even finding out what is wrong with them—but we medicine men can and we are able to cure such cases. A third type of illness is snake bite. You can cure that, and we Navaho also have our own medicines for that.[24]

Professionals who have worked with the Navaho have found that they are willing to adopt new ideas if these fit into their culture.

HASIDIM AND THE AMISH

Sects such as are found in inner-city Hasidic and rural Amish communities build sociological and psychological walls behind which they

[24] John Adair, Kurt Deuschle, and Walsh McDermott, "Patterns of Health and Disease Among the Navahos," *The Annals*, 311 (May 1957), pp. 8–94.

live out their lives. Inner-city sects live amid greater pressure to form interethnic relationships and are consequently in more precarious situations than most rural sects. Social controls have to be reinforced constantly to maintain the necessary boundaries for their stability. Because of the strong controls within such groups, it is unusually difficult for individuals to break away from ethnic sects.

Isolation has positive and negative aspects. Geographical separation, whether in the inner-city enclave or the rural village, rigidifies the system by cutting down the input and thus the potential for innovation. On the other hand, it insures the continuity of traditions from one generation to the other. In most such communities, however, some marginal people are beginning to build links with out-groups and can be considered agents for potential change.

The Hasidic community of the Williamsburg section of Brooklyn in New York City maintains strong internal controls and rigid boundaries despite its location in the heart of a rapidly changing urban environment. In this Orthodox Jewish group, concepts of health and illness are prescribed by the Talmud and the Torah. Health and illness emanate from a divine source, and men must pray continuously to stay well. "Every illness is the result of sin" is the precept. The written laws of the Talmud give explicit information about the body, based on observation of diseases and experiments on animals.

Paralleling this scientific approach to medicine is a rich stratum of folk-beliefs, documented in the Haggadah, that enumerate astrological remedies for diseases and preach redemption of the soul. Some Hasidic sects actively oppose scientific medicine and turn completely to prayer, but the majority of Hasidim, adopting the general attitude of Jews throughout the centuries, regard medical care as a religious obligation. The injunction appears in the Talmud: "He who refuses to heal is a shedder of blood."

Although among the modern Hasidim of Williamsburg physicians and rabbis work together, all important decisions about health must be mediated by the rabbi, who is an advocate for his group. Because of dietary and other restrictions, many treatment procedures and oral medications are prohibited, and this tradition prescribes a whole system of ritual conversions of medical equipment by immersion in holy water. There are rules for living and rules for dying.[25]

Although the Amish are also an isolated religious community, they are, in contrast, agriculturalists by preference. There is nothing

[25] Solomon Poll, *The Hasidic Community of Williamsburg* (New York: Schocken Press, 1969).

in Amish religious tenets that runs counter to modern medical practice. Yet the Amish do have a folk tradition of medicine. Unlike the Hasidim, the Amish maintain folk medical practices as a consequence of their isolation from modern medical care. When illness strikes, the Amish must resort to empirical knowledge, and they therefore cling to the old and tried traditions that they have come to trust more than science. The Amish, who value face-to-face associations, rely on the advice of friends rather than physicians. Because they reject higher learning, there are no Amish doctors.

The Amish operate on a selective principle, deciding in favor of modern medicine in situations of "sudden illness" and on folk medicine for chronic conditions. In the latter situation, sympathy healing or *brauche*, sometimes called "pow-wowing," is used. *Brauche* is performed by older Amish of the opposite sex who apply their special gifts of healing by the laying on of hands and incantations. There is great secrecy about these procedures, but the chief features are the recitation of verses and charms.[26]

In Amish society sickness is an accepted form of deviation, and the "sick role" is sanctioned, even rewarded. A concern for the sick is of major importance in every Amish community. Details about health become major news items. The Amish newspaper, *The Budget*, devotes long detailed columns to health issues and advertises a great many remedies for arthritis, constipation, "itch," and so forth. Some of the most prevalent conditions in Amish society are obesity, chronic bed-wetting after 6 years of age, digestive disturbances, and mental disorders, all of which are associated with stress.

SICILIAN AND GREEK-AMERICANS

Other ethnic groups with differing histories and different levels of social integration into American society present a range of challenges for modern western medical care. A recent study of Sicilian-Americans who settled in upstate New York has indicated they retain supernatural interpretations of illness and a system of local healers.[27] They sought the advice of both physicians and local curers, but the longer the illness continued and the greater the doubt about the diagnosis,

[26] John A. Hostetler, "Folk & Scientific Medicine in Amish Society," *Human Organization*, 22 (Winter 1963–64), pp. 269–275.

[27] M. Estellie Smith, "Folk Medicine Among the Sicilian-Americans of Buffalo, New York," *Urban Anthropology*, 1 (Spring 1972), pp. 87–106.

the greater became the inclination for folk curing. In this group two kinds of folk healers were identified: the *spilato* ("healer"), whose healing power is in his hands and who does not accept money for his services; and the *curandera* ("curer"), occasionally called a *strega* ("witch"), who uses herbs, medical brews, formulas, amulets, and so forth. Illnesses were described as resulting from the following causes: (1) curses from witches or other humans, (2) God's curse as punishment for violation of a moral or religious rule, (3) the *mallocchio*, an evil eye of an unintentional nature, and (4) *fatura,* an evil eye that is deliberate and in which the person is targeted as a victim. These beliefs were pervasive among the Sicilian-Americans in the area despite differences in education, occupation, religious commitment, and length of time in the United States.

Greek-Americans also have many traditions that are pertinent to medical practice even when they are not specifically medical traditions. Lee provides these notes on their style of living:

> The body image is the image of Greek character. Fortitude and hardihood, firm will, a love of simplicity in food, entertainment, furnishings are common traits. . . . A Greek takes no inventory of himself because from the time he was a baby, his parents saw to it that he grew straight and hard. . . . A current book on child care warns parents not to take many toys to a sick child, not to clown for his amusement, lest this spoil him. Going to bed also is a sign of weakness except for recognized disease. A man cannot seek solace in bed for fatigue or indisposition, lest he appear to be giving in; the term is, "sleep caught me!" [28]

In this culture, the eyes are the organ of greatest significance. Speech is also of extreme importance since it fosters personal relationships. At the same time, there are rigid regulations about covering the body. No delight is taken in a naked child of either sex. "Mothers often arrange to bathe and change the baby without undressing it all at once." [29]

There is a strong sense of family responsibility among Greeks, and obedience is taught to a child from birth. The Greek sense of individuality and freedom affects all his attitudes toward work, social relationships, and time.

[28] Dorothy Lee, *Freedom and Culture* (Englewood Cliffs, N.J.: Spectrum Books, 1959), p. 144.

[29] Ibid., p. 147.

To hurry is to forfeit freedom. People often arrive an hour late to an appointment to find that the other person is also just arriving, or, if they find him gone, they usually accept the fact with neither apology nor frustration.[30]

Some of these attitudes may be changing as succeeding generations interact with American institutions. Yet some of the more basic characteristics are perpetuated by the family and the social network. One can see how these might conflict with modern medical systems and cause misunderstandings, if they are not respected and incorporated into institutional planning.

Examples from other groups reinforce the fact that ethnic ways persist over time and that they bring great richness and diversity to American society. This paper has not discussed the curing traditions of black people, such as "the root doctors" of the South, or how such practices survive in city life. The complex problems of "ghetto medicine" have been documented by Norman.[31] They reflect similar situations among other impoverished minorities, which deserve separate studies.

INSTITUTIONAL MEDICINE

The fullest possible utilization of health services, whether in preventive medicine or in acute and chronic care, has been a primary concern of institutional medicine. Usually educational means or some other type of conditioning have been used to motivate patients to understand and agree with the values and objectives of the medical caretakers.

Social control factors in medicine have been repeatedly documented. Roth made the following observation:

Every institutional system which serves a client population seeks some degree of control over the behavior of the clientele. Insofar as this control is explicit, it is defended by the institutional agents with the argument that their institutional staff has an occupational expertise which enables them to establish rational procedures to better serve the relatively ignorant and inexpert persons who require their service. Such controls take the

---

[30] Ibid., p. 152.

[31] John C. Norman, ed., *Medicine in the Ghetto* (New York: Appleton-Century-Crofts, 1969).

form of rules and procedures designed to guide the clientele along certain paths and to prohibit other kinds of behavior.[32]

Roth's studies in five hospital emergency rooms located in the Northeast and on the West Coast revealed some of the techniques used to alienate or discourage a client population consisting primarily of ethnic poor; avoiding and ignoring patients, controlling priorities of treatment, selecting patients of interest to physicians, making patients wait too long, discouraging family and friends from accompanying patients, supporting them, or inquiring about them, withholding information, and asking irrelevant or embarrassing questions of patients. Experienced and aggressive patients learn to manipulate the system, and they wrest some control from hospital staff by complaining and by circumventing the rules. More assertive ethnics may be able to manage this effectively, but the newcomers or those who already feel alienated from the dominant society come to hospitals only when faced with critical situations and tend to drop out of ongoing care.

The medical profession in the United States assumes little responsibility for change. Instead, the people served are expected to conform to what organized medicine thinks medical care should be. People are supposed to learn to want what others who supposedly know better tell them they need. Western physicians define illnesses according to rational standards and western values. They define how people should act when they are ill, which illnesses are serious and which are not, and what type of care people in different socioeconomic brackets should be receiving. Professionals now decide such ethical questions as who shall live and who shall die.

American health care is a subsystem of the total society in the United States. It is an extreme example of the institutions that are dominated by the white upper-class elite who are in control throughout the society. Medicine screens novitiates who enters its ranks. These novitiates are molded and taught to conform to established codes, but there are, nevertheless, many who never lose the spark that motivated them to be curers. It is in this last sense that the medical system becomes a paradigm of conflict and contradiction. Authority, affluence, independence, power, rationality, proficiency, objectivity, standardization, complex corporate structures, and closed ranks all clash with caring, dedication, concern for social conditions, idealism,

[32] Julius A. Roth, "Staff and Client Control Strategies in Urban Hospital Emergency Services," *Urban Life and Culture,* 1 (April 1972), pp. 39–60.

and identification with the suffering of society. American medicine presents many paradoxes, and many physicians are undoubtedly burdened with conflicts and ambivalences, which they may be compelled to submerge or displace.

At present an interesting process is taking place. Organized medicine is being threatened from without by consumers, state and federal agencies, and private insurers. The fight is going to be as fierce as it was in the United Kingdom when health care was nationalized despite the bitter opposition of the royal medical societies. The fascinating aftermath of this battle is that physicians in the United Kingdom are now able to give the kind of patient care they had always wanted to administer. They are more concerned with social problems, and their status in British society has not diminished. People need them, respect them, and use them. This could be a lesson for America. Medical care could become more oriented to people and more authentic.

ADJUSTMENT TO CULTURAL PLURALISM

To determine what is dysfunctional about American medical care as it relates to ethnic groups, it is necessary to reevaluate certain assumptions. Perhaps the most important one has been the assumption that people should conform to the structures and schedules of the medical care system. The time has come to reverse this assumption. Institutions themselves must change—not the people who are served by them. There is a vital need to eliminate the system's dehumanizing and exclusionary practices by teaching medical personnel to become sensitive to the many rich cultures in this country and to respect their differences.

As Ehrenreich and Ehrenreich have pointed out, "It is necessary to see medicine as something other than what medical men themselves define it as." [33] One can add that it is necessary to define illness behavior as something other than what leading sociologists, such as Parsons, say it is. Cultural pluralism needs to become an added dimension in dealing with illness and health.

Medical professionals have so far not developed a sufficient respect for the strength of social networks in ethnic communities. The influence such networks have on how people use medical care may be

[33] Barbara Ehrenreich and John Ehrenreich, "Health Care and Social Control," *Social Policy*, 5 (May-June 1974), pp. 26–40.

even stronger than that of the medical institutions themselves. Friends and family are powerful obstructionists or motivators in decisions to seek or forego medical care. Freidson refers to the singular importance of the lay consultants who are interposed between the first perception of symptoms and the decision to see a professional.[34] Yet, modern medical institutions do everything possible to split the patient off from his supportive networks. If medical professionals could learn to understand and use the potentialities of the patients' support systems, they would enhance their power to cure. The lay referral system is not only used when people are deciding whether to consult a physician. Diagnoses and prescriptions are often discussed with "significant others," and this may be why some patients do not follow up on a physician's initial treatment.

This, then, illustrates another questionable assumption—that illness is the private concern of patients and doctors. This may be true in middle-class white families where individuality and privacy are primary values. However, in many ethnic groups, illness is a social event fully involving "significant others." An awareness of this fact could affect the way information is conveyed to patients, the involvement of families in caring for ill members, the structuring of hospital visiting time, and the development of policies concerning visiting children. At present, hospital personnel generally regard families as a "nuisance factor," as meddlers. There is relatively little thought of involving them except in dispositional planning.

ETHNIC EXPECTATIONS

The criteria used by ethnic groups to evaluate and choose physicians generally involve other qualities besides competence. The quality of the interaction between the physician and patient is vital. With local healers, the interaction is personal and has a social as well as a physical component. The patient is physically handled and given immediate treatment without elaborate diagnostic testing. Furthermore, he is listened to. However, the interaction between doctors and patients in most institutional settings is characterized by scientific detachment and jargon. Sensitivity training and the development of skills in interpersonal communication are not high priorities in modern medical education. This social distance can alienate those whose experiences

---

[34] Eliot Freidson, "Client Control and Medical Practice," *American Journal of Sociology*, 65 (January 1960), pp. 374–382.

are more familistic and group oriented. It can leave them dissatisfied and reluctant to use such services again.

Researchers at the Children's Hospital in Los Angeles studied interactions of eight hundred mothers with physicians. They found that the "language barrier was by no means the most serious bar to effective communications. . . . the most common complaint of the dissatisfied mothers was that the physician had shown too little interest in their concern about their child." [35] The mothers wanted sympathy and friendliness shown to them and to their children, but they felt instead that their concerns were disregarded. In summary, the study found that friendly treatment of the patient generally brought better results and insured a return for follow-up care.

Expectations of the physician-patient relationship vary along ethnic lines. The Chinese, for example, are said to expect doctors to be authoritative and are respectful toward those they see as having high status. Jews are said to be skeptical, demanding, and probing in their questions. Italians are typically more dependent and are appreciative of any relief given to them. Specific needs for supportive relationships which scientific medicine may regard as irrelevant, are of singular significance to community groups and affect utilization rates in institutions. The ethnocentrism of modern medical practitioners is dysfunctional in helping poor and ethnic populations. It is the culture of medicine rather than the culture of the patient that is the major impediment to the improvement of health in this country.

STRUCTURAL CHANGE

Several serious efforts to alter the structure of health delivery systems have been made. Community mental health and comprehensive medical care facilities at neighborhood levels have proliferated in the last decade. Health centers funded by the Office of Economic Opportunity (OEO) have demonstrated more utilization by the poor. These settings have used indigenous paraprofessionals, have practiced active outreach, and have created environments in which familiar symbols and local beliefs are not repudiated as irrelevant. An example of this in the area of mental health was the OEO health center in the South Bronx in New York City. The medical team there included anthropologists who identified the herbalists, faith healers, and mediums in

[35] Barbara M. Karsch and Vida Francis Negrete, "Doctor-Patient Communication," *Scientific American*, 227 (August 1972), p. 72.

the local Puerto Rican community.[36] In this center, local mediums were used to treat certain patients, and a pharmacopoeia of herbs used by the Puerto Rican therapists was compiled.

The sudden flowering of community free clinics, mostly staffed by medical students, came as a reaction against the formalism and impersonality of the medical bureaucracies. Despite the fact that they met a vital need and were overutilized by the community, they were criticized by the medical establishment as providing "second-rate" medicine and have gradually been disappearing.

All these efforts at the neighborhood level have one basic objective, that of fitting services into traditional frameworks. As a matter of interest, some of the more recent therapies, such as biofeedback, the therapeutic practice of meditation, the therapeutic use of hallucinogenic drugs, and now the application of acupuncture, have their origins outside the traditional frame of Western medicine.

The maintenance of health is a source of anxiety for all people, and different ethnic groups deal with illness in different ways. Adaptations to illness are conditioned by beliefs concerning the causes of ill health, and treatment rests consequently on these fundamental etiological explanations. Every known society has developed methods for coping with disease and thus has created a theory of medicine in keeping with its whole culture. Different groups vary in the degree to which they perpetuate their traditions. Those remaining segregated, whether by preference or exclusion, tend to adhere more rigidly to their folk traditions. Others, with greater openness in their systems, reach greater and more productive levels of syncretism between the traditional and the modern. In the United States, where ethnic groups live contiguously and where interchanges are fairly continuous, few groups have been able to preserve the purity of their traditional systems. Even if rational medicine is convinced that it has a better approach to curing illness and maintaining health, it could still recognize that its effectiveness depends on a willingness to address itself to the "ethnic imperative." This requires that it open its organizational system to the diversity of ethnic life-styles.

[36] E. Fuller Torrey, *The Mind Game* (New York: Emerson Hall Publishers, 1972), pp. 145–146.

American Indian Tribal Support Systems and Economic Development

LEONARD D. BORMAN

Leonard D. Borman, Ph.D., is Director, Self-Help De-velopment Institute, Center for Urban Affairs, North-western University, Evanston, Illinois. At the time this essay was written, the author was Program Director, W. Clement and Jessie V. Stone Foundation, Chicago, Illi-nois.

EDITORS' COMMENT

Research has shown that ethnic and racial groups whose cultures closely resemble that of the majority society are more successful economically than groups whose cultures are dissimilar. The more different the culture of the ethnic group, the more difficult it is for that group to achieve economic success. Because they reflect the majority society, Germans and Swedes, for instance, tend to be economically successful as well as accepted by mainstream America. The value system of the American Indians, however, differs greatly from that of the

Europeans who settled in this country. An examination of American Indian culture in relation to government policies shows the need for radical adaptations of social policies and programs to reflect community values.

Social policies should reflect the uniqueness of North American Indian culture as manifested in its distinctive systems of human values, the patterns and preferences of the several hundred tribes, and the organization of tribal life. In the past, however, federal governmental policies have weakened, rather than strengthened, traditional tribal mechanisms for handling individual and community matters. Borman recommends a community development corporation model for economic development among North American Indian tribes. Such a model recognizes the corporate, communal basis for development and places the governance in the hands of the local community.

In recent studies conducted by behavioral scientists and human service practitioners, the importance of indigenous support systems has been increasingly recognized. Caplan, a psychiatrist, compared the "natural" support system to the professional support system. The former, including family, kinship, ethnic, self-help, and mutual aid groups, provides important psychological support as well as concrete advice and value clarification, which not even the best psychotherapy can replace. These systems provide opportunities for emotional development and for guidance in dealing with everyday stresses; they supply meaningful feedback that can steer individuals in realistic directions.[1]

Similar findings have emerged in the work of Shimkin and his associates with black communities in Mississippi, Louisiana, and Illinois. They have documented an extended family system, operating over five generations, that has strengthened the capacity of local black communities to manage many problems without bureaucracies, agencies, and professionals.[2] Other studies—including those of Gartner

---

[1] Gerald Caplan, *Support Systems and Community Mental Health* (New York: Behavioral Publications, 1974). *See also* Leonard D. Borman, ed., *Exploration in Self-help and Mutual Aid* (Evanston, Ill.: Center for Urban Affairs, Northwestern University, 1975).

[2] Demitri Shimkin, Gloria Louie, and Dennis Frate, *The Black Extended Family* (The Hague: Mouton & Co., 1976).

and Riessman, Mowrer, Warren and Clifford, Hurvitz, and Gussow and Tracy—are interpreting the role of kinship, group, community, consumer, and other corporate support networks in society.[3]

Glazer has reasoned that the chief cause of America's social problems has been the breakdown of traditional arrangements vested in the family, the ethnic and neighborhood group, and the voluntary association. In focusing on the recent increase in abandoned families on welfare rolls throughout the country, Glazer concludes that the solution to such social problems can be found in revitalizing traditional practices and restraints. Such a revitalization, he contends, provides planners with two forms of guidance in dealing with the hazards of modern life:

> First, it counsels hesitation in the development of social policies that sanction the abandonment of traditional practices; and second, and perhaps more helpful, it suggests that the creation and building of new traditions must be taken more seriously as a requirement of social policy itself.[4]

TRADITIONAL LIFE

Although none of these studies, including Glazer's policy recommendations, was based on observations of North American Indian tribes, the situation of North American Indians certainly corroborates their findings. Current observations and experiences of both Indians and non-Indians are leading to the recognition that the distinctive systems of values and organizational forms of North American Indian tribes

---

[3] Alan Gartner and Frank Riessman, *The Service Society and the Consumer Vanguard* (New York: Harper & Row, 1974); O. Hobart Mowrer, *The New Group Therapy* (Princeton, N.J.: D. Van Nostrand Co., 1964); Donald Warren and David L. Clifford, *The Decision to Seek Help: A Pathways Approach to Mental Health Services Delivery* (Ann Arbor, Mich.: Institute of Labor and Industrial Relations, University of Michigan, 1974, mimeographed); Nathan Hurvitz, "Peer Self-Help Psychotherapy Groups: Psychotherapy Without Psychotherapists," in Paul M. Roman and Harrison M. Trice, eds., *Sociology of Psychotherapy* (New York: Jason Aronson, 1974); Zachary Gussow and George S. Tracy, *Voluntary Self-Help Organizations: A Study in Human Support Systems* (Department of Sociology, Louisiana State University, 1974, mimeographed).

[4] Nathan Glazer, "The Limits of Social Policy," *Commentary*, 54 (September 1971), pp. 51–58.

still flourish. Although these values and forms are often unnoticed by outsiders, they remain vital and meaningful as underpinnings to American Indian communities throughout the continent.

It may be difficult for many people steeped in Western traditions to understand the Indian ways of life. In great part this may be due to the policies of the federal government, which were not de· signed, in Glazer's sense, to protect Indians. Instead, they almost completely annihilated Indian societies and cultures. Vogel, in dealing with the treatment of the American Indians in school texts, points out that Indians are usually obliterated, disembodied, defamed, or disparaged.[5] Motion pictures have contributed to this defamation. There is little wonder, then, that this country has what Vogel calls a "blackout" toward American Indian culture. At the same time, Indian ways are in great dissonance with prevailing Western ways, and, consequently, many Westerners encounter psychological and social barriers to a full appreciation and understanding of Indian culture.

It may not be too late, however, to seek a fuller understanding of the traditional practices and patterns that are still cherished by contemporary North American Indians. Prompted by Glazer's guidance, this effort may reveal ways to abandon or revise policies that tend to destroy traditional practices and structures. It is to be hoped that, with the leadership and involvement of Indians themselves, more equitable and workable social policies can be fashioned. In formulating social policies, the unique patterns and preferences of North American tribes must be recognized, and policy suggestions for economic development must be congenial with Indian traditional ways. As a Sioux holy man once stated, "It may be that some root of the sacred tree still lives. Nourish it then, that it may leaf and bloom, and fill with singing birds." [6]

It is in matters of economic development and making a living that the key values and social structures of Western man become most pronounced. The emphasis in Western society is on the individual, who is urged to develop a career, a calling, or a profession—to make something of himself. The time orientation is the future, watching the clock, thinking ahead, planning for the next day or month or year. The Western notion of "progress" involves development, change, improvement, and especially individual achievement. Freedom is the

---

[5] Virgil J. Vogel, *The Indian in American History* (Chicago: Integrated Education Association, 1968), pp. 1–8.

[6] John G. Neihardt, *Black Elk Speaks* (New York: Simon and Schuster, 1973), p. 233.

emancipation from all the ties that hold people to their present place or position or condition. Local ties can be burdensome if one seeks to reach the "executive suite."

The impersonal world in which one learns to function is often governed by arbitrary rules, regulations, laws, and procedures. The authority structures resemble pyramids, with orders filtering down from the top to those below. Furthermore, one is surrounded by specialists trained in technical fields for which they are ranked, classified, and compensated accordingly. This is the world of the "position description," which specifies duties, responsibilities, and areas of authority. Individuals in this system must be relatively mobile, equally substitutable, and available to work almost anywhere.

Local community ties must be kept tenuous and impersonal, for one's economic activities are separate from one's social, religious, family, and community obligations. Each of these is carried out in the company of different persons, with the economic round of life assuming priority. Money becomes an important measure of all things and an object sought almost as an end in itself.

This caricature of Western economic man stands in great contrast to the image of a traditional North American Indian. Anthropologist Rietz, who worked closely with American Indians in North Dakota and Iowa and was Director of the American Indian Center in Chicago, recalled this story that made the contrasting values rather dramatic:

> We in effect tell them [school children] a little story. We know a fellow who didn't have any more money than they did, and worked hard and saved everything he got. Everyday after school he stayed home and studied and studied more. And he learned more and more and more. He went through high school and during that time he worked in the cafeteria, and he went on to college and worked in the cafeteria, and he took on jobs to make more money and so on. He kept on studying and working hard and graduated from college, and eventually he went to medical school and he became a doctor. And we think by telling this little story, or by offering this possibility, that we are offering them a kind of encouragement. Well, frankly, to tell this to some of the traditional Indians is to tell them an incredibly selfish kind of story. Here is this fellow who paid attention to no one but himself. All he worried about was what he was doing for himself. He shut himself off from everybody, he was worrying and stewing and spending all of his time figuring out what he was going to get and what he was going to do and he didn't even go to visit anybody and he didn't take part in any of the group's ceremonies or activities. He didn't do anything but concentrate on his own personal private welfare. What kind of fellow is this? The point

involved here is that the simple communication which we think we are effecting is simply not there; there is a different definition of this behavior. It does not exist on the same terms, the listener and the speaker. We are talking about two different things literally; two different kinds of things are happening.[7]

Economic and personal success in the Western tradition, as this story indicates, often involves the progressive alienation of the individual from family and community ties. When a child is asked, "What are you going to be when you grow up?" he is being prodded to start thinking about his own future calling, about "making something of himself." His eventual separation from family, community, or neighborhood may be painful but is regarded as inevitable and desirable—by Western people, but not by American Indians. The question "What are you going to be . . . ?" makes little sense to American Indians. Becoming "something" or "someone" implies, among other things, that one is "nobody" now and that one's identity lies somewhere off in the future, in a special profession, a particular community, or a higher class.

It may be difficult for Westerners to understand that the pulse of American Indian life continues to beat at the local community level of extended family kinfolk bound to one another in face-to-face relations.[8] These extended families are the basic units within their tribes, and unlike Western nuclear families, they have an important function in the governance of the larger unit. Tribal leadership is traditionally made up of family heads.

> One must say American Indian tribes rather than "Indians" because the identity of an individual member is dependent, in a way difficult for urban people to understand, upon that of his tribe. A person is a Zuni or Navaho; a Mohawk or Seneca; a Cherokee or Choctaw; Hupa or Pomp; a Cheyenne or Crow or Oglala Sioux; or one of the hundreds of other nations, tribes or bands. Non-Indian is a useful term; but "Indian" is both the classical mistake of Christopher Columbus and a misconception of secular, urbanized non-Indians whose families are part of large,

[7] Robert Rietz, "Culture, Identity, and the Self," p. 9. Paper presented to the staff of Veterans Administration Hospital, Downey, Illinois, 1959.

[8] Vine Deloria, Jr., *We Talk, You Listen* (New York: Dell Publishing Co., 1970); and Robert K. Thomas and Albert L. Wahrhaftig, "Indians, Hillbillies and the 'Education Problem,'" in Murray L. Wax, Stanley Diamond, and Fred O. Gearing, eds., *Anthropological Perspectives on Education* (New York: Basic Books, 1971).

impersonal populations of classes, religions and ethnic groups. The family and religion of tribal man are his tribe; his home is the land where in the beginning of the world the tribe was born, where everything important happened, where the spirits dwell and the ancestors are buried.[9]

For most traditional Indians, the choice between employer and community or between a career and a continuing kinship relationship is usually clear. For a traditional Indian, the personal accumulation of money or worldly goods as ends in themselves makes little sense. If an individual Indian succeeds materially, he is expected to share his wealth with members of his tribe.

The dissonance caused by these values can be quite painful, especially in urban America. The author recalls an incident: An American Indian in Chicago, who worked as a boilermaker, traveled daily in car pools with non-Indians. He did not feel he had much in common with his fellow riders, who spoke with pleasure of their washing machines, garbage disposal units, lawn mowers, weed killers, and— most startlingly of all—of the thirty- to forty-year mortgages they were paying on their houses. "Can you imagine," he said, "tying yourself to future debts in this way. You might have to work forever in a cruddy job with an s.o.b. for a boss just to pay off your house." This Chicago Indian believed his home to be in Wisconsin with his tribe and saw his stay in Chicago as temporary because this was where he could find employment.

FEDERAL POLICIES WEAKENED TRIBAL LIFE

The intent of most federal policies developed for American Indian tribes was to weaken rather than strengthen traditional tribal mechanisms for handling individual and community matters. Individuals were separated from their families, families from their tribes, and, perhaps most devastating of all, tribes from their land. In less than a hundred years—from 1887 to 1966—Indian land held in trust diminished from 138 to 55 million acres. The terms used in the policies reflect the reality of the government's intentions for the Indians: removal, assimilation, termination, relocation, allotment, and the like. The early programs of education for American Indian youngsters often transferred the children from their families and tribes to inaccessible boarding schools. Speaking native languages was forbid-

[9] Sol Tax, Foreword to Virgil Vogel, *This Country Was Ours* (New York: Harper & Row, 1972).

den. These schools were often surrounded by barbed-wire fences to keep the youngsters from running away.

While the cultural and social ties to one's tribe were being severed, few paths were opening up to the urban industrial life of America. Thomas and Wahrhaftig have described the conditions that prevailed for the Cherokee of eastern Oklahoma:

> In a stagnant rural area, berefted of both farming and industrialization, with serious problems of unemployment and, because of migration, an under-representation of competent young adults, there is no ladder of occupations linking folk-like country communities and the new middle class. Only those individuals who can make the behavioral adjustment to working in a service industry, dependent on the good will of an impersonal middle-class clientele, are assured mobility; and no sequence of occupations exist that allow Cherokees and folk Anglo-Saxons to experience the behavior that pleases middle-class consumers.[10]

Sometimes programs regarded as humane and thoughtful, programs that were conducted by sincere and dedicated individuals, proved to be the most disastrous. Rietz once described the introduction of a new hybrid corn to an Indian tribe. He thought the story may have been apocryphal, but it made an important point. A high yield corn had been developed and tested by the Department of Agriculture and was already being used extensively throughout the country and indeed the world. The seed of this hybrid corn produced full-bodied, even, yellow rows of corn. It could survive severe weather conditions and was regarded as the most productive variety available. The Indians were initially responsive, according to Rietz. They looked kindly on efforts to grow demonstration plots of this corn and listened attentively when the hybrid variety was compared with the kind the Indians had been growing for years. The Indian corn produced a small number of tough, often gnarled kernels. The yield was smaller and the nutritional value was far less than the new hybrid variety. The government offered to provide free seeds of the new corn to anyone who wanted them. When the Indians finally responded, they explained some facts to the agent that they thought he did not know. They admitted that his variety was more nutritional and provided a higher yield than their own. But they also explained, "We are the people that grow this corn." Their ancestors had always lived on the same land and had always grown this variety of corn, which was associated

---

[10] Thomas and Wahrhaftig, op. cit., p. 245.

with special dances, songs, and costumes. "If we don't grow our corn anymore, who are we?" they asked.

This story caused Rietz to be more cautious in recommending programs to American Indians and to question current proposals for economic development that were alien to the values of the people.

> You see, on the one hand, you can be an urban type like me and say, well, there are X number of people and this is X number of acres and the rainfall is such and such and it's located on the so and so, and so on. You are talking about a productive unit, which is an abstraction. You talk about people there, really, as abstractions, producing units, what they need to consume, effort and manpower, work they have to put in to get this kind of return. And you apply this simple mathematical scheme and you come up with this ear of corn and everything ought to move. Anybody who uses reason ought to literally take that little thing [the Indian corn] and save it for a souvenir and plant this big corn. And at that level, the problem is kind of simple. What he said was "we're the people who plant this corn." Now what he is trying to tell me is not what he does to maximize his personal resources and merge them with group efforts in order to bring about the greatest possible production per working unit. He is trying to tell me who he is. He is not telling me something about a list of resources that they have that they don't propose to lose or anything else. He is telling me an answer to the big question. There is only one big question. Who are you? What are you? And he is getting down to rock bottom. This is not a big theoretical statement that he gave me. This is down on the bottom where life is. He is telling me, "Mr. Rietz, we're the people who plant this corn. That's who I am." [11]

Another important perspective that Rietz was attuned to but that eludes most people was the American Indian's view of Western man. John Mohawk, a Turtle Clan Seneca, presented such a view recently at a gathering of American Indians concerned about their treaty rights. Mohawk pointed out that the Spanish who came to North America learned about Indians from Sepulveda, who taught in Spain. He held that the Indian people in North America were not really people, that they were "an inferior kind of people, without souls, without intelligence," who "do not speak Spanish or Latin, . . . build cities, . . . follow the writings of the Bible, . . . [or] educate

[11] Robert Rietz, "Culture, Freedom, and the American Indian Centers," pp. 6–7. Transcription of talk presented at workshop of American Indian students, Boulder, Colorado, 1965.

their children." They were, he maintained, "natural slaves, . . . born to serve us, the Spanish." [12]

Although some of the rhetoric has changed, many of the Western patterns vis-à-vis the American Indians have persisted. The Citizen's Advocacy Center, which monitors governmental programs, maintains that current federal government Indian policy frustrates self-realization, makes dependency a virtue, and rewards alienation. The center has researched and reported in great detail the ways in which the Bureau of Indian Affairs (BIA) governs the lives of over six hundred thousand American Indians living on and off reservations.[13]

The BIA, unique among federal agencies, is the federal, state, and local government of the Indians. It supplants or dominates the private sector as well by assuming the roles of realtor, banker, teacher, and social worker. It runs the employment service, the vocational and job training program, contract office, chamber of commerce, highway authority, housing agency, police department, conservation service, water works, power company, telephone company, and planning office. It also functions as land developer, patron of the arts, ambassador from and to the outside world, guardian, and spokesman.

Headquartered in Washington, D.C., the bureau has sixteen thousand employees scattered in outposts across the country. The BIA commissioner has his own cabinet in Washington. The bureau consists of sixty departments or branches in charge of community services, economic development, education, administration, engineering, and program coordination. This structure is duplicated on the regional level in area offices, headed by area directors. It is duplicated a third, and even a fourth, time at the reservation—or agency and subagency —level. Behind every official looking over every Indian shoulder, there are several layers of officials looking over each other's shoulders. The authority of the bureau in every realm of Indian life is absolute, both as a legal and practical matter. Cahn summed the alignment up this way:

> Although the normal expectation in American society is that a private
> individual or group may do anything unless it is specifically prohibited
> by the government, it might be said that the normal expectation on the

[12] John Mohawk, "Working for a Good Life for Our People," *Akwesasne Notes*, 6 (July 1974), p. 6.

[13] Information available from the Citizen's Advocacy Center, an affiliate of the Center for Community Change, Washington, D.C.

reservation is that the Indians may not do anything unless it is specifically permitted by the government.[14]

The situation of the North American Indians, particularly in the United States, reveals that federal public policies, when they were no longer directed at annihilating the Indians, continued to weaken their traditional societal structures. Impersonal public authorities replaced traditional tribal ones. This pattern results, as Glazer points out, in the weakening of traditional sources of support and

> . . . further encourages needy people to depend on the government, rather than on traditional structures, for help. Perhaps this is the basic force behind the ever growing demand for social policy, and its frequent failure to satisfy the demand.[15]

COMMUNITY DEVELOPMENT CORPORATIONS

In recent years, a number of suggestions have come forth that would reverse the historical policies. One promising direction may produce economic development opportunities for American Indians at the same time that it strengthens tribal and communal ways. Essentially, this involves combining the philosophy of the earlier Indian Reorganization Act (IRA) with current efforts to establish community development corporations.

The IRA was developed as federal policy in the 1930s to promote Indian self-government and economic development. The IRA attempted to stop the non-Indian acquisition of Indian land. The IRA placed reservation land under tribal ownership. This was the first time the right of Indian tribes to be self-governing was recognized, although questions were raised, mostly by Indians, about whether Western majority-rule democracy did not alienate consensus-seeking tribal procedures. Tribal councils were organized, model constitutions developed, low-interest loans made available, and tribal investments and enterprises encouraged. However, these initial efforts at communal self-governance were no longer encouraged after World War II. The Secretary of the Interior wielded a heavier hand in controlling tribal activities; legislation for the termination of the federal jurisdiction of Indian tribes was initiated, and the period of relocating Indians

---

[14] Edgar S. Cahn, ed., *Our Brother's Keeper: The Indian in White America* (New York: World Publishing Co., 1969), pp. 7–8.

[15] Glazer, op. cit., p. 54.

to urban areas began. Since 1968, termination and relocation have been deemphasized and policies encouraging greater self-determination and Indian control have surfaced once again.

A principal instrument outlining the requirements of this new policy has been the community development corporation (CDC), which was described in a recent Ford Foundation policy paper as

> ... a locally controlled, tax-exempted corporation that operates programs aimed at both immediate relief of severe social and economic disad-vantage and at eventual regeneration of its community. Its programs are usually funded by grants or investments from government and the private sector; and they seek primarily to increase jobs and income, and to improve housing and to secure better services from local governments, business, and utilities, and to foster a sense of hope in communities that have been stagnant or deteriorating.[16]

While the foundation proposal for community development cor-porations was not developed primarily with Indian communities in mind, it represents a model that Indian tribes may find congenial. The policy paper, which calls for an outlay of foundation funds in the amount of $75 million over five years, recognizes the failure of earlier government efforts to support small businesses in disadvantaged areas.

> These frequently marginal and dispersed enterprises cannot carry the burden of redevelopment. Experience so far indicates that programs aimed mainly or exclusively at small business development seem to have little institutional impact in disadvantaged communities.[17]

Bills proposing federal support for community development cor-porations have been submitted to Congress on several occasions. The Community Self-Determination Act that would charter CDCs was introduced in Congress in 1968 but was not passed. Likewise, the Community Corporation Act of 1970 failed to gain the required majority. Nevertheless, according to the Ford Foundation report, there are well over one hundred local agencies in the United States that claim to be community development corporations, and this does not count the over one hundred tribes organized under the IRA. Some CDCs have been supported and assisted by the Ford Foundation,

---

[16] "Community Development Corporations: A Strategy for Depressed Urban and Rural Areas." A Ford Foundation Policy Paper (New York: The Ford Foundation, 1973), p. 5.

[17] Ibid., p. 7.

others by special programs of the Office of Economic Opportunity and the Model Cities Program. Future legislative support may expand these efforts and apply CDC principles, technical assistance, and funding to American Indian tribes. This effort might be combined with current movements among American Indian tribes to regain title to lands now under federal jurisdiction and trusteeship.

Deloria, a staunch advocate of such efforts, sees community development corporations as a new form of tribalism for modern urban man. CDCs would become holding and development corporations. Income, as it was handled traditionally, would revert to tribal or corporation programs—thus combining the usually distinct profit-making and nonprofit activities. Policies, programs, and new enterprises would be developed by the local tribe or corporation and carried out by elected officials responsible to the people of the local community or corporation. Deloria points out further similarities between CDCs and Indian tribes:

> The tribe operates as a community of individuals in its elective processes. Its main concern is the ongoing life of the community, and thus it has an undifferentiated view of its economic-social-political-religious problems. . . . The CDC (under recent legislation) would place the voting franchise at the age of sixteen and anyone in a local area to be served by a community corporation is eligible to vote to determine its policies and programs. This provision bridges the generation gap in the local communities in a much more realistic manner than society has tried to do with its national voting franchise. . . . The genius of the CDC is that it recognizes that all elected and appointed officials must be responsible to the people they are hired to serve. . . . A bureaucrat must account to local people after hours, informally, and continually since he must live in the neighborhood that he serves.[18]

The CDC model seems compatible with Western ways as well as Indian ways. CDCs recognize the corporate, communal basis for development, which is similar to the traditional tribal support system. They permit governmental change and development to occur through the initiatives of the community itself, not through the top-down planning of outside experts. They place the essential initiative for economic development and social improvement in the hands of the community. The hope is that outside resources, technical knowledge, and capital will become more accessible—but as servants of the local community and not as its master.

[18] Deloria, op. cit., p. 7.

It is obvious that the Bureau of Indian Affairs needs to be drastically revised if CDCs are to succeed. American Indian tribes can, as they have in the past, find their own solutions to current problems only if some of the needless barriers to full community functioning are removed. The community-development corporation model may provide one way for this to occur, not only in American Indian communities, but in other ethnic communities as well.

Bilingualism in America

PASTORA SAN JUAN CAFFERTY

*Pastora San Juan Cafferty, Ph.D., is Assistant Professor,
School of Social Service Administration, University of
Chicago, Chicago, Illinois.*

EDITORS' COMMENT

Bilingualism is central to any notion of a pluralistic society. Since language and culture are closely aligned, it is important to analyze the complexity of a society that, although describing itself as pluralistic and claiming acceptance of other cultures, has, through its educational policies, imposed English monolingualism on its citizens. The conflict the assimilation model poses for the immigrant is examined by Greeley, who establishes the model's limitations in explaining the process of Americanization. May establishes the difficulties that being different from the mainstream of American society poses for the individual. The individual who speaks a language other than English is considered the least assimilated and, thus, is isolated from the mainstream.

By retaining their native language, sometimes to the exclusion of English, Spanish-speaking immigrants have confirmed their isolation and delayed their assimilation and acceptance. Chestang would view them as developing in a hostile environment that demands linguistic adaptation as the price of acceptance. However, the reality of their migration and the geographical proximity of their respective homelands have made native-language retention necessary for survival in the nurturing environment. The Spanish-speaking, as a group, have had the greatest incidence of native-language retention in this country.

Among the Puerto Ricans, at least, language retention is due to a cyclical migration between two monolingual societies, Puerto Rico and the United States. Educational policies that deny the reality of this problem and fail to educate bilingual individuals are evidence of the insistence of American society on perpetuating an assimilation model and its refusal to acknowledge the reality of cultural and linguistic pluralism.

American society has defined its ethnic plurality in various ways. Hector St. John de Crevecoeur, author of the popular tract *Letters from an American Farmer,* described "the American, this new man" in terms befitting an eighteenth-century pastoral romance:

> He is neither a European nor the descendant of a European; hence that strange mixture of blood, which you will find in no other country. . . . *He* is an American, who, leaving behind him all his ancient prejudices and manners, receives new ones from the mode of life he has embraced, the new government he obeys, the new rank he holds. He becomes an American by being received in the great lap of our Alma Mater. Here individuals of all nations are melted into a new race of men, whose labours and posterity will one day cause great changes in the world.[1]

Americans have repeatedly defined this society of immigrants in terms of an assimilation of various cultures into a new, distinct one. From the earliest days of the republic, public policies have reflected and fostered the assimilation of European immigrants. Although in the case of Orientals, blacks, and American Indians assimilation was discouraged through segregation and exclusion, American society demanded from everyone some form of assimilation in language and custom.

[1] Hector St. John de Crevecoeur, *Letters from an American Farmer* (New York: The New American Library of World Literature, 1963). pp. 63–64.

Since 1786, when the United States Congress adopted English as the only official language, the immigrant's proof that he had assimilated —that he had become an American—has been his ability to speak English. Early public education policy in this country was founded on educating the immigrants to be "good Americans." That being a "good American" was often defined as the ability to speak English explains why English language instruction was the earliest form of adult education in the twentieth century. Although knowledge of English did not become a requirement for citizenship until 1940, American society did not support the efforts of immigrant groups to preserve their language and culture. The pervasiveness of this assimilationist view from the earliest days of the republic down to our own day is responsible for the paradox that America, a nation that originated from a variety of linguistic traditions, is monolingual.

Language is the most utilized expression of a culture and its traditions. Since language and culture are inextricably united, it might be assumed that a society that calls itself a "nation of immigrants" and extols the contributions of a variety of ethnic groups would encourage linguistic expression of that cultural pluralism by fostering the retention of the native tongues of its immigrants. In fact, the opposite is true. Bilingualism in America is highly dysfunctional. The speaking of English as the native tongue has long been associated with the opportunities for social and economic advancement.

In spite of assimilation, each group of immigrants has attempted to preserve its culture and its linguistc identity. The success of these efforts, in direct opposition to a national policy of monolingualism, is dramatic proof of the immigrant's need to preserve his native culture while becoming part of the new American society.

LANGUAGE AND CULTURE

Language as a catalyst in preserving culture is not unique to America. It is the history of every society. Organized language consciousness, language loyalty, and language maintenance by different ethnic groups in the Western world have a history of over five centuries.[2] In this hemisphere, the preservation of native languages by the indigenous inhabitants of South America reflects the preservation of those ancient cultures. In countries such as Ecuador and Peru, where the native

[2] Joshua A. Fishman, *Language Loyalty in the United States* (London: Mouton & Co., 1966), p. 25.

culture plays a vital contemporary role, particularly in remote mountain areas, the indigenous languages are preserved, often to the exclusion of the national language, Spanish. Canada has a long history of bilingualism, reflecting the political and cultural division between its French and English citizens. It was largely the fear of such political division and domestic dissension that created monolingualism in America.

Strains of ethnocentrism and nativism at different periods in American history reflect a derision and fear of "foreign" languages and accents. Those immigrants unable to speak and write English were classified as illiterate and, often, as ignorant and were subjected to social and economic sanctions.

In spite of this philosophy of linguistic and cultural assimilation, immigrants maintained foreign language schools and presses, attesting to the need of the individual and the community to maintain the native language and culture. There were more bilingual education programs prior to World War I than there are today. The xenophobia and nativism that followed that war greatly reduced the number of bilingual programs as well as the number and circulation of the foreign language presses.

Native language retention varies among ethnic groups, but its presence recurs throughout American history. As late as 1960, approximately 19 million Americans (11 percent of the population) spoke a language other than English as their native tongue. They read 500 non-English newspapers and periodicals published in the United States, with a circulation of 5.5 million and an equally large "pass-along" readership. They listened to 1,600 non-English radio stations, two-thirds of which broadcast in Spanish.[3]

The Spanish-speaking have the greatest rate of native language retention in the United States.[4] Among the Mexican-Americans of the Southwest, this can be attributed to their proximity to Mexico and to Mexican migrant workers, as well as to the isolation and exclusion imposed by the English-speaking society.[5] Spanish has been preserved for two centuries by the descendants of the Mexicans who inhabited the Southwest territories annexed after the War of 1845. There is evidence that the preservation of native language and culture in America is greatest in rural areas, where migrants were isolated and,

[3] Ibid., p. 392.

[4] Jane Macnab Christian and Chester C. Christian, Jr., "Spanish Language and Culture in the Southwest," in Fishman, op. cit., p. 286.

[5] Ibid., p. 287.

perhaps, forced to continue communicating in their native tongue. This may account for the initial retention of Spanish language and culture in the Southwest.

BILINGUALISM AMONG PUERTO RICANS

The phenomenon of the retention of Spanish among Puerto Ricans on the mainland, along with an increase of English in Puerto Rico and the growth of "Spanglish" or "the language of the barrio," is a new one in American society. This bilingualism among Puerto Ricans, with its reflections of cultural pluralism and implications for educational policy, is worthy of examination. It testifies not only to the needs of the 1.3 million Puerto Ricans on the mainland and the nearly 2.7 million on the island, but to the larger question of ethnic diversity and cultural pluralism in contemporary America.

Puerto Rican migration to the United States dates to the nineteenth century when the island was still a Spanish colony. Puerto Rico ranks along with Ireland in having had one of the highest rates of emigration ever to characterize a country. In contrast to Ireland, however, Puerto Rico industrialized and urbanized rapidly during the period of its massive out-migration. And unlike the Irish, Puerto Ricans have left and returned to their small island throughout their migration history.[6]

The Puerto Rican migration experience is drastically different from the European. The laborious journey that brought the European to America made him different from his fellow villagers who stayed in Europe. By making that journey the immigrant affirmed his desire and conviction to become an American.[7] The Puerto Rican makes no such pilgrimage. He boards a plane in San Juan to arrive in New York only a few hours later, knowing that a week's wages will buy him a ticket home. Puerto Ricans, citizens of the United States under the complex commonwealth status of the island, do not cross frontiers when they come to New York, although certainly the customs and values of the mainland are foreign to the islanders.

Puerto Rican migration to the mainland reached its greatest pro-

---

[6] Jose Hernandez Alvarez, *Return Migration to Puerto Rico,* Population Monograph Series, No. 1 (Berkeley, Calif.: University of California Press, 1967), p. 7.

[7] Oscar Handlin, *The Uprooted* (Boston: Little, Brown & Co., 1951), pp. 37–62.

portions in the 1950s, when almost half a million Puerto Ricans settled on the mainland.[8] In 1945 nonscheduled airlines began offering one-way tickets to New York City for as little as $35, and in some instances the cost could be paid in installments after arrival in New York. According to the 1950 census, there were slightly over 75,000 persons born in the United States of Puerto Rican parentage. The census also records 226,000 immigrants, so that the first and second generations together numbered approximately 300,000. By 1960, the census recorded almost 900,000 Puerto Ricans in the United States, with a ratio of roughly 2 persons born in Puerto Rico for every Puerto Rican born on the mainland.[9] By the mid-sixties, at least 1 of every 3 persons born in Puerto Rico had lived in the United States at some time.[10] About this time the drastic decrease in the outflow of migrants and the rapid increase in return migration began to assume importance in the social and economic life of the island.

RETURN MIGRATION

This trend toward return migration has continued, so that between 1965 and 1970, 198,696 persons living on the mainland returned to Puerto Rico. The social significance of this increases when it is realized that the number of returnees more than doubled between 1963 and 1968. Roughly two-thirds of all those returning live in urban areas of the island.[11] More than 120,000 Puerto Ricans had lived more than five years on the mainland; of these, 73 percent reside in urban areas of Puerto Rico.[12]

The shorter stay of rural workers on the mainland is explained by the seasonal farm work they perform, an explanation that may not apply to those returning to urban areas. A survey conducted at San Juan International Airport during the period from 1957 to 1964 indicates that a large number of Puerto Ricans returning to the island expect to stay for some time. Many respondents said they had

[8] *Annual Report* (San Juan, Puerto Rico: U.S. Immigration and Naturalization Service, 1965), p. 6.

[9] Alvarez, op. cit., p. 5.

[10] Ibid., p. 40.

[11] U.S. Department of Commerce, Bureau of the Census, *United States Census of Population: 1970*, Vol. 1, *Detailed Characteristics of the Population* (Washington, D.C.: U.S. Government Printing Office, 1973), Tables 55 and 78.

[12] Ibid.

returned to find work. The theme of returning to settle on the island —implying some permanence—was also evident.[13]

The characteristics of the return migration substantiate this fact: the close ratio of male to female returnees and the age of those returning suggests that it is mostly families, not itinerant workers, who return to the island.[14] The fact that men and women tend to stay proportionately the same length of time on the mainland suggests that many of those returning are family units. This is further substantiated by the median age of those returning, 25 years of age. Furthermore, approximately one-third of the 129,105 returnees who were living on the mainland in 1965 were children and adolescents under 19; over half were of childbearing age, between 15 and 45 years old; and only 4,496 were of retirement age, over 65 years old.[15]

The fact that the Banco Popular de Ponce in the Bronx does a lively business selling homes to Puerto Ricans who want to return to the island might suggest that Puerto Ricans retire to spend their old age on the island. However, census figures show that, in fact, only a small number do so. The majority who go back return to raise families. This arouses speculation. The traditional belief throughout American history is that immigrants come to give their children a future in the new land. Yet Puerto Ricans return while their families are still young and of school age. A recent study performed for the city of San Juan on the problem of the return migrant in the San Juan public schools documents that thousands of children in the metropolitan schools do not know Spanish. It is estimated that an equal number in the public schools outside the metropolitan area have language problems.[16]

BURDENS OF MONOLINGUALISM

The problems this creates for the school systems of Puerto Rico are obvious. Puerto Rico had generally not taught English as a second

[13] Bureau of Labor Statistics, *Characteristics of Passengers Who Traveled by Air Between Puerto Rico and the United States, Fiscal and Calendar Years, 1957–64* (San Juan, Puerto Rico: Commonwealth of Puerto Rico, Department of Labor, 1966).

[14] U.S. Department of Commerce, Bureau of the Census, op. cit., Tables 55 and 78.

[15] Ibid.

[16] Privately circulated report, San Juan, Puerto Rico, 1974. Mimeographed.

language in its public schools since 1948 until a few bilingual programs were instituted in the 1970s. Although many Puerto Ricans
speak English, and this is considered an indication of upward mobility,
children are expected to speak, read, and write Spanish in school.
Puerto Ricans are as devoted to their Spanish language and culture
as English-speaking Americans are insistent on their monolingual
society. There are no bilingual programs for the large numbers of
returnees, so that these English-speaking children are either ignored
or placed in the lower grades where they can learn Spanish with first-
and second graders. A generation of Puerto Rican children on the
mainland has dropped out of the public schools because of frustration over the denial of Spanish culture and language and their inability to compete with their English-speaking classmates. Now their
counterparts on the island, Puerto Ricans born in New York and
Chicago, share the same fate because they do not know Spanish!

The Puerto Rican child has not fared well in school. In 1970,
Puerto Ricans 25 and older had completed 8.5 years of school, which
puts them 4 years behind Chicanos in educational achievement. In
that same year, only 20 percent of the Puerto Ricans over 25 had
finished high school.[17] In Chicago, 71.2 percent of the Puerto Ricans
dropped out of school.[18] In Boston and Cleveland, the rate was over
90 percent.[19]

The dropout problem has long been attributed to the Spanish-
speaking child's inability to learn English. However, a study of Puerto
Rican dropouts in the Chicago public school system argues that
"problems of self-concept caused by discrimination, difficulty in
relating to their parents, and progressive estrangement from the
school were more important factors in influencing the rate." [20] There
was no positive correlation between knowledge of English and high
school graduation. Indeed, a higher percentage of the Puerto Rican
high-school graduates indicated they knew Spanish better than English,

---

[17] Federal Interagency Committee on Education, *Task Force Report on
Higher Education and Chicanos, Puerto Ricans, and American Indians*
(Washington, D.C.: U.S. Government Printing Office, April 1973), p. 19.

[18] Task Force on Education, *National Research Project on the Dropout
Problem: Spanish-Speaking America* (Washington, D.C.: Cabinet Committee
on Opportunity for Spanish-Speaking People, March 1973), p. 18.

[19] Samuel Betances, "Puerto Ricans and Mexican Americans in Higher
Education," *The Rican,* 1 (May 1974), p. 33.

[20] Task Force on Education, op. cit., p. 18.

while more dropouts indicated they knew English better.[21]

Bilingualism and nationalism are highly complex phenomena. Historical evidence indicates that nations with a variety of native languages and a poorly established national language have long and stormy histories of ethnic warfare. However, Kloss points out that there is no reason why a nation state should resist bilingualism so long as one official language is spoken by everyone. That one official language, he stresses, will be sufficient to insure unity if newcomers are truly bilingual; that is, if they speak both their native language and the official language. Only if bilingualism does not prevail and newcomers retain their native tongue to the exclusion of the national language, does dissension arise.[22]

The policy of English monolingualism in America has been justified for almost two hundred years on the assumptions that immigrants who came to stay in America became citizens and that their children would become a new generation of native Americans. To aid the assimilation process, each generation of new immigrants and their children were encouraged to learn the new language and the new ways.

MOTIVES FOR MIGRATING

Although there is no doubt that many still come to America to seek freedom of conscience, the majority seem to be looking for a better life through economic opportunity. It is futile to argue what complex motives led the European immigrant to settle in an unknown land, but from the beginning many came in search of work. And many of those who found it returned home with their earnings. From as early as 1860, there are reports of workers from Lancashire, iron molders from Scotland, and coal miners from other parts of the United Kingdom returning home. Some immigrant groups had a higher rate of return than others. For example, most of the Irish stayed, while hundreds of thousands of British workers came and went, reflecting economic cycles.[23] Italian workers form a stream that ebbs and flows

[21] Isidro Lucas, *Puerto Rican Dropouts in Chicago: Numbers and Motivation* (Washington, D.C.: U.S. Office of Education, March 1971), p. 13.

[22] Heinz Kloss, "Bilingualism & Nationalism," *Journal of Social Issues,* 23 (April 1967), p. 45.

[23] Clarence Senior and Donald O. Watkins, "Toward a Balance Sheet of Puerto Rican Migration," *United States-Puerto Rico Commission on the Status of Puerto Rico* (Washington, D.C.: U.S. Government Printing Office, 1966), p. 692.

from Italy to America, so that in 1903 more than 98,000 Italians returned home. And by 1904, 134,000 more had returned to Italy.[24] It is interesting that most of the returning immigrants were of the laboring classes. Ravenstein points out that "the net migration in any direction is but a fraction of the gross migration in the same direction . . . each main migrating current has associated with it a countercurrent." [25]

Most Europeans came to America to find the promise of a better economic life. Puerto Ricans also migrate for higher wages and better employment opportunities, as do most Americans traveling within national borders. Evidence indicates, however, that Puerto Ricans do not define life in the barrios of New York and Chicago as better. Indeed many give the search for a "better life" as their reason for returning to Puerto Rico.[26] So the movement between the island and the mainland does not demand commitment to a new language or a new identity. It is cyclical, requiring each individual to possess an understanding of the two languages spoken in the two monolingual communities between which he travels.

There is no sense of leaving the homeland for another country—only of travel to the north. In fact, Puerto Rican migration is really no different from the travel of highly mobile Americans from one city to another. It would be foolish to challenge the millions of Americans who move yearly to change their language or linguistic patterns in order to become acceptable members of society. Yet, this is what American society asks of the Puerto Rican who is only traveling from one American city to another.

IMPLICATIONS FOR BILINGUAL EDUCATION

The confusion imposed on an individual Puerto Rican by the two monolingual societies, each demanding that he conform to one language and culture, is most damaging to the children. The importance of self-identity in determining a child's educational achievement

---

[24] John Foster Carr, "The Coming of the Italians," *Outlook,* 82 (1966), pp. 426–427.

[25] E. G. Ravenstein, "The Laws of Migration," *Journal of Royal Statistical Society,* 48 (June 1885) , p. 167.

[26] George C. Myers and George Masnick, "The Migration Experience of New York Puerto Ricans: A Perspective on Return," *International Migration Review* (Spring 1968), p. 85.

has long been known. An extensive study shows that pupils who move frequently between educational institutions even within the same city tend to do worse than their counterparts who remain in the same school.[27] That language is crucial in determining self-identity is acknowledged by most sociolinguists.

An extensive study of French-Canadian children in New England shows that the bilingual, bicultural individual can suffer from divided linguistic and cultural loyalties. However, if he can successfully integrate the two, they can be a source of strength for him and for the society. The study used a series of attitude scales to assess the allegiance of these French-Canadian–American adolescents to both their French and American heritages. The youths were divided into four groups: (1) those who preferred American to French culture and spoke English better than French but who expressed anxiety about the quality of their spoken English, (2) those who stressed their French cultural heritage and spoke French far better than English, (3) those who were confused and ambivalent about their allegiance to values of the two cultures and lacked fluency in both languages, and (4) those who seemed equally comfortable in both cultures, had great aptitude in both languages, and manifested acceptance of other cultures.[28] This study, as well as a number of others, testifies eloquently to the desirability of bilingual education for children whose native tongue is not English.

BILINGUAL EDUCATION PROGRAMS

In spite of the knowledge that bilingual education would be eminently helpful to the five million American children having a non-English mother tongue, such programs are few in number. It was not until 1967 that Congress passed the Bilingual Education Act. The seventeen states that have legislation and appropriations for bilingual education view their programs primarily as tools for teaching English. There is no state or national effort to educate bilingual individuals

[27] Thomas S. Smith, *Consequences of Pupil Mobility Within the Inner City* (Chicago: University of Chicago, Department of Sociology, Center for Social Organization Studies), p. 20.

[28] Wallace E. Lambert, "A Social Psychology of Bilingualism," in Roger D. Abrahams and Rudolph Troike, eds., *Language and Cultural Diversity in American Education* (Englewood Cliffs, N.J.: Prentice-Hall, 1972), pp. 197–200.

to become equally fluent in both languages. The acquisition of a second language by American children whose native tongue is English is considered a cultural asset, as is evidenced by the foreign language requirements of high schools and colleges. The retention of a foreign language, on the other hand, is seen as a cultural detriment.

Thus, there is no policy to foster bilingualism. Bilingual education programs merely acknowledge the fact that children can learn English better through the use of their mother tongue. The recent enactment of bilingual education legislation is not a change in a national policy but an educational innovation to better foster monolingualism.

Since language is the articulation of cultural identity, many would argue that if an individual cannot articulate his native identity by using his mother tongue that identity is imperiled. Furthermore, analysis of seventy-six bilingual projects financed through the Office of Education in 1968 under the Bilingual Education Act indicated that a child who was taught English through his native language learned quicker and retained that knowledge better than those in monolingual programs. Children in these bilingual programs also did better in all other subjects. When a person studies a subject in a language he knows only imperfectly, he will not do as well as those who are fluent in that language. His poor performance usually has direct correlation with his dropping out of school later.[29]

Appropriations for the Bilingual Education Act were relatively small, but the act had significant impact because it gave respectability to the concept of bilingual education, which was eventually paired with bicultural education. The history of Title VI of the National Defense and Education Act (NDEA) presents an interesting contrast to that of bilingual education legislation. Title VI of the NDEA established language and area centers and programs "for the teaching of any modern foreign language, for instruction in other fields needed to provide a full understanding of the areas, regions, or countries in which such language is commonly used. . . ."[30] It was not until ten years later that the Congress would enact bilingual education legislation to meet "the special educational needs of children of limited English-speaking ability." These children are defined as "children who came from environments where the dominant language is other

[29] Garland Cannon, "Bilingual Problems and Developments in the United States," *Publication of the Modern Language Association*, 86 (May 1971), p. 456.

[30] *National Defense Education Act, United States Code*, vol. 17, sec. 511 (1967).

than English." [31] Children who know a language other than English are classified as children of "limited English-speaking ability," and Congress makes provision authorizing the use of federal funds to develop bilingual programs only in those schools "having a high concentration of such children from families (a) with income below $3,000 per year, or (b) receiving payments under a program of aid to families with dependent children. . . ." [32] The children whose native language is other than English are seen as the children of the poor, who must learn English to achieve the economic promise of America.

Nowhere in the bill is the retention of the mother tongue described as a primary purpose of the bilingual programs. Nowhere is it affirmed that the mastery of two languages is a cultural asset of benefit to American society as is assumed in the National Defense Education Act. National policy, as enacted by Congress, asserts that it is good for Americans to acquire other languages. Since 1958, $347.5 million has been appropriated under NDEA Title VI for foreign language instruction, including $150 million for fiscal years 1974 and 1975. [33] In contrast, only $35 million was appropriated in 1974 for the Bilingual Education Act.

THE ETHNIC HERITAGE PROGRAM

Congress approved the historic Ethnic Heritage Program as part of the Education Act of 1972. The program was approved:

> In recognition of the heterogeneous composition of the Nation and of the fact that in a multiethnic society a greater understanding of the contributions of one's own heritage and those of one's fellow citizens can contribute to a more harmonious, patriotic, and committed populace, and in recognition of the principle that all persons in the educational institutions of the Nation should have an opportunity to learn about the differing and unique contributions to the national heritage made by each ethnic group. . . . [54]

The Ethnic Heritage Program recognizes the heterogeneous composition of American society and authorizes federal funds "to afford to students opportunities to learn about the nature of their own cultural

---

[31] *U.S. Code Annotated,* Sec. 880b and following (Supp., 1975).

[32] Ibid., Sec. 880b (b)(1).

[33] *U.S. Code,* Sec. 511 (1958).

[34] *U.S. Code,* Sec. 900 (1972).

heritage, and to study the contributions of the cultural heritages of other ethnic groups of the nation." [35] In essence, this congressional recognition of a pluralistic society is not in conflict with Crevecoeur's description of American society two hundred years ago or with the great "melting pot" described in early twentieth-century pageants. Americans have always been proud of being a nation of immigrants. The Ethnic Heritage Program merely provides funds for American children to learn more about the contribution of immigrants. The thrust of the program is for developing, testing, and disseminating materials for elementary and secondary school curricula. Creation of these materials will involve oral histories, graphic arts, and social and demographic analyses.

The essence of American pluralism, of a nation of immigrants who are the children of two cultures, will not be realized until Congress and state legislatures make provisions to ensure the retention of the native languages, which are the articulation of the native cultures. For the Spanish-speaking in America, who have remained a bilingual people, such legislation would be a recognition of the fact that they live in two cultures and that for them, at least, the American experience must be an integration of the two.

Such national policies should base eligibility for federal funds on the percentage of a school district's population speaking a native language other than English, rather than define such eligibility according to society's guidelines. It should encourage the teaching of the other languages to native English-speakers within the district, and it should provide funding to compensate for the long neglect of the Spanish-speaking in the nation's schools.

3M—11/76—P.C.

[35] Ibid.